JEREMY WALKER

EP Books (Evangelical Press), 1st Floor Venture House, 6 Silver Court, Watchmead, Welwyn Garden City, UK, AL7 1TS

admin@epbooks.org
www.epbooks.org

Distributed in the USA by: JPL Books, 3883 Linden Ave. S.E., Wyoming, MI 49548

order@jplbooks.com
www.jplbooks.com

ISBN

Print 978-1-78397-205-0

Kindle 978-1-78397-206-7

What people are saying about this book:

The brevity of this work betrays its significance. Rarely have I been so challenged and encouraged by a single book. It is demanding and convicting, and yet instructive and hopeful. Like a compass, it turns the reader back to the heart of true discipleship. Initially, it deserves multiple readings, and then, it should be read once a year to help the believer maintain the course.

Paul Washer, Founder and Missions Director
of HeartCry Missionary Society

This is a great little book that is much needed at the present time, written by a real man of God for whom I have huge respect. It considers the Lord Jesus Christ as he sets out on his way to Jerusalem to accomplish our salvation. The Lord Jesus of the Bible, the one to whom this book points us, is what a real man should be: clear-eyed with unflinching determination, conviction, self-discipline and courage. But he is not cold or stoic. To quote Jeremy, "Christ had a face like flint because he had a heart on fire." I recommend this book enthusiastically and pray that we will have the same flint-like determination to seek God, make our salvation sure, put sin to death, increase in holiness, be godly husbands, wives, fathers, mothers, children, church members, and to carry out whatever we have been called to carry out for the kingdom.

Alun Ebenezer, Headmaster of Fulham Boys School, author

Jeremy Walker has provided us with a valuable treasure in this new book, *A Face Like a Flint*. Writing with an engaging pen, he does a masterful job of describing for us the unflinching resolve of the Lord Jesus Christ as He headed to the cross. This same firm determination is so desperately needed in our lives today. In a day when many believers are lacking depth of convictions, this book will put a backbone of steel into followers of Christ as we walk in His steps. Be ready to be challenged by what you read and compelled to live with the same unwavering fortitude as did our Lord.

Steven J. Lawson, President, OnePassion Ministries

In a culture where casual Christianity dominates so much of evangelicalism, a prophetic voice is needed to call true believers to a holy determination to follow Jesus. Jeremy Walker in this book is that voice. *A Face Like A Flint* powerfully points us to the redeeming work of Jesus and his unchanging word as the key for every Christian to channel this righteous tenacity. Written with a clarity, wit, and precision that mark all of Walker's books, you will be inspired and convicted to pursue Christ, cling to his word, and hold fast until the end with a renewed resolve. I commend this book and the faithful man who wrote it.

Brian Croft, senior pastor of Auburndale Baptist Church, founder of Practical Shepherding, and Senior Fellow of the Church Revitalization Center, SBTS

Thomas Watson wrote: "Zeal does not say, 'There is a lion in the way'. Zeal will charge through an army of dangers, it will march in the face of death." Jeremy Walker's book is a clarion call for that kind of zeal. Looking to our Redeemer as our Example, and the Scripture as our authority, he aims an arrow at the heart of a casual and complacent generation of Christians, and his aim is true. His book reads like a sermon. It really is "logic on fire". It is passionate, pointed, practical and pastoral. If we hear and heed his words, we shall be better, and more useful, servants of our God. I, for one, shall be praying for a wide and receptive readership for this much needed book.

Carl Muller, pastor of Trinity Baptist Church, Burlington, Ontario

The Apostle John recorded, "The one who says he abides in [Christ] ought himself to walk in the same manner as He walked." *A Face Like A Flint* shows Jesus as worthy to be worshipped as well as imitated. Walker's care and concern for both Christ's glory and people is evident as he reveals a clear path for the Christian life.

Anthony Mathenia, pastor of Christ Church, Radford, Virginia

Dedication

To those quiet and unknown saints, some of them friends of mine, who serve our God with a face like a flint.

CONTENTS

1. A face like a flint 11

The Lord Jesus fixed his eye on the goal 14

The Lord Jesus counted the cost of the way 17

The Lord Jesus pursued his path to the end 19

2. Salvation Secured 29

The Lord Jesus grasped his identity 31

The Lord Jesus embraced his activity 34

The Lord Jesus anticipated his victory 38

3. Grasping the goals 45

A principled commitment 48

A righteous choice 50

A steadfast conviction 51

4. Counting the cost 63

The matter of the Christian's concern 65

The vigour of the Christian's conviction 67

The intensity of the Christian's cry 71

5. Pursuing the path 81

The believer's resolution 82

The believer's direction 84

The believer's expectation 87

A FACE LIKE A FLINT

Have you ever been righteously surprised, even scared, by a righteous man? Have you been shaken by his righteousness? The disciples of Christ knew what it was to have such an experience.

Has your fiercely holy disposition, your commitment to a righteous cause, ever troubled anyone else? Have you ever righteously surprised or scared someone? The Lord Jesus did. He did it as he went up to Jerusalem to lay down his life on the cross, as Mark records:

> Now they were on the road, going up to Jerusalem, and Jesus was going before them; and they were amazed. And as they followed they were afraid. Then He took the twelve aside again and began to tell them the things that would happen to Him: 'Behold, we are going up to Jerusalem, and the Son of Man will be betrayed to the chief priests and to the scribes; and they will condemn Him to death and deliver Him to the Gentiles; and they will mock Him, and scourge Him, and spit on Him, and kill Him. And the third day He will rise again.' (Mark 10:32–34)

The spirit that broke the surface of Christ's life on that occasion can be seen again in a similar setting earlier in his life. Luke records it in the ninth chapter of his Gospel: 'Now it came to pass, when the time had come for Him to be received up, that He steadfastly set His face to go to Jerusalem' (Luke 9:51—the parallel to Mark 10 is in Luke 18:31-34). There is something here of the disposition of which the prophet Isaiah spoke, when he spoke the words of God's Servant:

> The Lord God has opened My ear; and I was not rebellious, nor did I turn away. I gave My back to those who struck Me, and My cheeks to those who plucked out the beard; I did not hide My face from shame and spitting. For the Lord God will help Me; therefore I will not be disgraced; therefore I have set My face like a flint, and I know that I will not be ashamed. (Isaiah 50:5–7)

Here, God's Messiah, in the face of many sufferings, set his face like a flint. This, says Matthew Henry, was a disposition of 'unshaken constancy and undaunted resolution; he did not fail nor was discouraged.'[1] Can you not imagine something of that look in the eye of the Lord Jesus when he cleansed the temple on various occasions? Can you not see it in his face as he throws mobs of liars and cheats out of his Father's house? Do you remember him standing in the building with a whip of cords, daring anyone to set back up what he had just torn down? His was a spirit of holy determination and righteous defiance and unashamed holiness. The God-man not only draws out our deepest love; he demands our utmost respect.

Now, in Mark 10, Christ and his disciples are on the road to Jerusalem. It is a long and steep climb up to the city. The Lord sets a fast pace, walking ahead alone. He outstrips his disciples. The

---

[1] Matthew Henry, *Matthew Henry's Commentary on the Whole Bible: Complete and Unabridged in One Volume* (Peabody: Hendrickson, 1994), 1176.

language suggests unusual energy and protracted activity. He both sets out and goes on rapidly. When the disciples look into his face they see a man with a certain expression, a certain look in his eye, a certain vigour in his actions. It is a portrait of a man not be messed about with. This is certainly the message received by the Twelve, and perhaps by others. They were amazed. The words can mean that they were astonished, frightened, even terrified. They and perhaps the crowd were struck with fear to the point of hesitation about following him. Perhaps some were even tempted to run away. They are deeply troubled. Jerusalem is the centre of the storm and they can see the clouds gathering and hear the ominous rumble of thunder. Opposition to and resentment against Jesus of Nazareth has been flowing from Jerusalem. The Lord Christ is now marching toward the city, striding into the heart of the storm, with an unsettling intensity, a frightening determination, a zealous eagerness. They do not know how to handle this. Christ has already made it very clear to the disciples that wherever and to whatever the Master goes, his disciples must follow: 'Whoever desires to come after Me, let him deny himself, and take up his cross, and follow Me. For whoever desires to save his life will lose it, but whoever loses his life for My sake and the gospel's will save it' (Mark 8:34–35 ff.). There is a sense in which they can see what is coming, and they are fearful as their Master cuts a path into the heart of the battle.

Perhaps taking note of all this, the Lord Jesus uses an interlude in the journey to spell out to the Twelve what lies ahead. It is a graphic and unflinching portrait of the betrayal, indignity and suffering to death that he must undergo, with the glorious vindication that will follow at his resurrection.:

> Behold, we are going up to Jerusalem, and the Son of
> Man will be betrayed to the chief priests and to the

scribes; and they will condemn Him to death and deliver Him to the Gentiles; and they will mock Him, and scourge Him, and spit on Him, and kill Him. And the third day He will rise again.

We must leave aside for a moment the immediate aftermath of this teaching. There the disciples display a quite staggering inability or unwillingness to grasp the Master's spirit and enter into his example. Our focus is on that spirit and example. We will concentrate on the convictions, character and conduct of Christ Jesus our Lord at this point, as an encouragement to us and a pattern for us. If there is a rebuke to us, we must take that too, and learn again what it means to follow Christ. We must look to Christ with his face like a flint as he marches up to Jerusalem.

❧

THE LORD JESUS FIXED HIS EYE ON HIS GOAL

The development of our Lord's self-awareness as Messiah is a deep river to sound. There are hints at the speed and the substance of that development as early as Luke's record of his appearance as a boy in the temple, when he asked his worried earthly parents, 'Why did you seek Me? Did you not know that I must be about My Father's business?' (Luke 2:49). It is characteristic of the Lord. As soon as he becomes aware of who he is, there is a constraint upon him: he has come to do his Father's will. Certainly this more than suggests a close to full-fledged grasp on his identity as the Son of God and the Son of Man. It also hints at the activity bound up in that identity. Later in life he is entirely aware of who he is, where he is going, and why he is going there: 'For even the Son of Man did not come to be served, but to serve, and to give His life a ransom for many' (Mark 10:45). He is fully determined to lay down his life in order to save his people from their sins. That conviction is written on to every page of the Gospels. He has his eye firmly fixed on his substitutionary, saving sacrifice. He is convinced that he must bear the cross before he can wear the crown. He is also persuaded that he will accomplish his task, as his assurance of the resurrection suggests: 'they will condemn Him to death and deliver Him to the Gentiles; and they will mock Him, and scourge Him, and spit on Him, and kill Him. And the third day He will rise again' (Mark 10:33–34).

The Lord Jesus knows exactly why he is going to Jerusalem. He is marching up to accomplish salvation through a substitutionary sacrifice. God is going to be glorified in Christ's death on behalf of his people. Those people are going to be blessed as he pours out his life's blood for them. And as he sets his eyes on the city, everything in him is concentrated upon that purpose, conscious of the fearful price to pay. His whole being is bent upon and consecrated to that great and glorious goal of securing the salvation of his chosen people.

Where did our Lord obtain such clear views of his work? How did he answer those questions about his identity and activity? Where he did he get that distinctive vision and sense of purpose? From the Word of God illuminated by the Spirit of God. His is a thoroughly biblical conception, derived from the humble and diligent study of the Scriptures of the Old Testament. Christ drew from the Bible his sense of his being, his calling, his working. We see again and again, in the titles he chooses, the allusions he frames, the connections he identifies, the references he makes, how entirely his consciousness of himself and his work is formed by divine revelation. Think, for example, of his public declaration of himself in his own town of Nazareth. He alone could fully enter into the words of the psalmist: 'Behold, I come; in the scroll of the book it is written of me. I delight to do Your will, O my God, and Your law is within my heart' (Psalm 40:7-8 cf. Hebrews 10:7). And so he goes, according to his custom, into the synagogue on the Sabbath day, and he is handed the scroll of Isaiah.

> And when He had opened the book, He found the place where it was written: 'The Spirit of the Lord is upon Me, because He has anointed Me To preach the gospel to the poor; He has sent Me to heal the brokenhearted, to proclaim liberty to the captives and recovery of sight to the blind, to set at liberty those who are oppressed; to proclaim the acceptable year of the Lord.' Then He closed the book, and gave it back to the attendant and sat down. And the eyes of all who were in the synagogue were fixed on Him. And He began to say to them, 'Today this Scripture is fulfilled in your hearing.' So all bore witness to Him, and marvelled at the gracious words which proceeded out of His mouth. And they said, 'Is this not Joseph's son?' (Luke 4:16–22)

He holds up the heavenly writings and finds in them what God calls him to be and to do. When he testifies that he must be about his Father's business, when he draws attention to the fulfilling of prophecies, when he expounds to his disciples in all the Scriptures the things concerning himself (Luke 24:27), it is because he sees in the pages of his Bible—at least, in the words of his scrolls!—his own portrait. From this he traces out his identity and his purpose in coming into the world.

THE LORD JESUS COUNTED THE COST OF THE WAY

The Lord Christ did not adopt a blithe and careless approach to his life. This is not a matter of blind ignorance, wilful or otherwise. He did not wander along this road and discover a few potholes and speed humps. He did not look at those obstacles and shrug and trip as he stumbled over them. He identified his goal and pursued it with full understanding of all that was involved both along the way and in the final accomplishment of that goal. Mark records Christ's deliberate and calculated survey of all the agonies required in his combat. It is a detailed prediction of the cost of victory. He knows that he will lay down his life as a ransom for many, betrayed by his friends, handed over by his people, abused in every way by his enemies, dying in drawn-out violence. We should not imagine that the assurance that he would rise again meant that all that lay between Christ and the cross was less than nothing in his sight. Yes, for the joy that was set before him, he endured the cross and despised the shame (Hebrews 12:2). However, you need only to stand for a moment in the Garden of Gethsemane as the burden of duty and the weight of sin drives him to the ground to understand the real pressure that all this exerted upon him. The physical and spiritual realities bow him down to the earth, crush him into the dust of the planet that he made. Nevertheless, we do learn that none of this was done ignorantly or involuntarily. He knew perfectly well what he was getting into. He knew every drop of blood to be shed, every blow that would fall, every stroke of the hammer, every moment of agony. He knew it would come to pass, and he went of his own free, determinate and deliberate will.

Christ not only fixed his eye on the his goal. He also knew every obstacle and hindrance, every pain and misery, each hurdle and all costs, that lay between him and his goal. Where did he

17

identify these obstacles? He warned his disciples about the need to consider such things. They needed to understand what was involved in following him.

> For which of you, intending to build a tower, does not sit down first and count the cost, whether he has enough to finish it—lest, after he has laid the foundation, and is not able to finish, all who see it begin to mock him, saying, 'This man began to build and was not able to finish.' Or what king, going to make war against another king, does not sit down first and consider whether he is able with ten thousand to meet him who comes against him with twenty thousand? Or else, while the other is still a great way off, he sends a delegation and asks conditions of peace. So likewise, whoever of you does not forsake all that he has cannot be My disciple. (Luke 14:28–33)

The Master and the disciples have this in common. So, how did he know? How did he calculate the cost? The same way he determined the basic duty itself. It was from the pages of the Book. The Word of God, his Father's revelation, brought and illuminated by the Holy Spirit, showed him both the way and the end. Again, he could ask his disciples on the road to Emmaus, 'O foolish ones, and slow of heart to believe in all that the prophets have spoken! Ought not the Christ to have suffered these things and to enter into His glory?' (Luke 24:25–26).

THE LORD JESUS PURSUED HIS PATH TO THE END

Christ had his eye fixed on his ultimate goal and his mind accurately full of all that lay between his present position and his final destination. With his heart full of all that lies before him, he strides out to Jerusalem. What do the Scriptures say? Again, read the Letter to the Hebrews:

> Therefore we also, since we are surrounded by so great a cloud of witnesses, let us lay aside every weight, and the sin which so easily ensnares us, and let us run with endurance the race that is set before us, looking unto Jesus, the author and finisher of our faith, who for the joy that was set before Him endured the cross, despising the shame, and has sat down at the right hand of the throne of God. For consider Him who endured such hostility from sinners against Himself, lest you become weary and discouraged in your souls. You have not yet resisted to bloodshed, striving against sin. (Hebrews12:1–4)

That is the very spirit expressed here! His eye was clear, his face like flint, his heart warm, his step sure, his stride long. He marches all the way to Jerusalem. He pressed on toward the goal in a spirit of committed obedience and holy determination—a principled intention to do what was right in the face of all obstacles and costs. He remained faithful to the very end of his costly path, pressing through all the sorrows and agonies before him in order to obtain his goal. In doing so, he brought glory to God and blessing to men, not to mention the securing of joy for his own holy soul, the favour of his heavenly Father. His willingness to go does not mean that the path was easy or pleasant. He nevertheless pressed on fiercely in order to obtain the prize.

How did he walk this way? Do you not wonder? What might you have done? So many of us flake out when presented with nothing more than a gentle incline with the promise of a breather at the top. Jesus climbed a mountain to die for others. Smooth downhill slopes are so much easier than rocky uphill paths. Living seems so much the preferable option to dying. But Christ's character had been forged on the anvil of revelation under the hammer strokes of God's Spirit. He lived as an obedient man, subject to all the directives and demands and duties that the Scriptures laid upon him, in dependence on and sustained by the Spirit of the living God.

Christ's conviction and our salvation

Have you ever seen such burning conviction? Have you ever met a righteous man who surprises and even scares you by the depth of his certainty and the degree of his determination to carry out the will of God? If you had never before seen this burning conviction worked out, I think it would have surprised and even scared you, too. Have you ever shown such burning conviction? It is a spirit that is all too rare today and is therefore all the more precious. But this attitude is often seen as some kind of abnormality, a freak of spiritual nature. Such convictions and actions are seen as something unusual, perhaps the mark of the fanatic, or at least of the manifestly odd. I do not believe that the Lord Jesus thought so. I believe that Jesus thought of this as the spirit of a true disciple, because it was the spirit of the Master.

We must correct a possible and dangerous mistake at this point. We are *not* calling for men and women of cold iron! We are of different constitutions and not all of us will manifest this spirit in the same way. Some of us might be inclined to find in this an excuse for a harsh or insensitive spirit. Some might excuse themselves because they do not have a forceful disposition. Some of us might be afraid that we will be trampled by those whose personality is naturally more dominant or aggressive. But this should never be a lever for any man or woman to become a bully or to entertain a critical or dismissive sneering. This is never to be a shallow veneer to cover the desire to get your own way or a readiness to crush the consciences of others. Christ had a face like flint because he had a heart on fire. His holy determination and principled zeal were and are the fruit of love to God and to men. This is not Christ seeking his will, his way. It is Christ seeking God's will, God's way, and pursuing it to the end at the greatest personal cost. At the same time, we do not deny that the manifestation of such a spirit can burn those who prefer their Christianity tepid. Nevertheless, it is not wildfire, and should never be imagined to be such. It is the light and heat of a man of God subject to the Word of God depending on the Spirit of God to be who God calls him to be and to do what God calls him to do.

This is the spirit in which salvation was secured. It is the spirit in which Christ our Lord went to the cross and sacrificed himself for others, delivering his people from the pollution, punishment and power of sin. Where would we be today if Christ had turned back when the path became steep or the end became dark? What would my prospects be if the pains and woes in Jerusalem had turned him aside? This spirit carried our Saviour to the cross of Calvary to save us from our sins. This is the heart and this is the face of the Good Shepherd as he lays down his life for his sheep. His eyes are clear and yet full of pain as he marches ahead of his flock to die for them. There is a sense in which we could and should look into the eyes of Christ at this point, and shudder at what he willingly embraced. Are you surprised at the fear of the disciples? Does this spirit scare you? It might! This is the Righteous One on his righteous course

—a ready obedience to the Father's will, a consuming zeal for God's glory, a burning love for his people's souls, a fierce hatred of sin. It carries him to give his life as a ransom for many. Without this, there would be no salvation for us.

This is also the spirit in which salvation is obtained. This purchased salvation is the life that is held out in Christ Jesus. Do you desire it? How much? To some, eternal life seems to be a thing of little moment and light weight. Speak of salvation to many, and they seem able simply to shrug it off as something of no real or abiding concern. It is a tragedy that there is no concern about being saved from sin and death and hell. People can sit in churches under the earnest, plain and loving ministry of God's Word, their minds shackled by spiritual darkness, and show no regard for these things. People can skim their Bibles and evade every exhortation and avoid every warning. People can read books about Christ's work of salvation and our need of it, and remain seemingly untouched. But there is a fearful condemnation for the wicked, and I pray that God would rouse you out of your slumber if he has not yet done so. Salvation is not a thing to be lightly esteemed, but a reality to be pursued at all costs.

To someone who is under the conviction of sin, instructed from the Scriptures as to his or her true state and feeling that fearful state under the influence of the Holy Spirit, nothing else matters but obtaining this salvation. Such a person is ready to seek the One who saves in much the same spirit as Christ seeks the ones who are lost. Christ calls sinners like us to obtain life in him. Christ tells us what that way involves. To come to Christ will be a momentous and even a costly thing. You must cast off pride. You must let go of sin. You may need to leave behind your reputation. You must put away your sinful pleasures. But—whatever the cost—you must be saved! You must give up anything that stops you coming to Jesus

22

Christ. If you are a Christian, perhaps you remember that sense, almost desperate in some cases, of the need to obtain peace with God? Perhaps you have never yet felt it? But whatever it demands, whatever price must be paid, we must set our faces, and press on and pray on until we have got Christ as the object of our faith. Nothing should hinder us or prevent us—we must seek Christ till we obtain Christ. Whatever it might cost us now or in the future, we must set out to gain Christ until we come to Christ. This is the spirit in which Christ saved his people, and it must be the spirit in which we go to him to be saved.

Saved and striving

Salvation is secured for us and obtained by us in this spirit. But this is also the spirit in which salvation as a whole is advanced. I ask again, have you ever surprised or even scared someone by your holy determination as a child of God? This is not a question of a Christian doing something else, adding something more to their roster of duties. It is about doing what is right and proper in the right spirit. Like the incarnate Christ himself, we need scriptural instruction, spiritual illumination and spiritual invigoration in order to fix our eyes upon our God-ordained goals, to count the cost of the way, and to pursue our path to the end. In the whole scheme of salvation, this is to be our spirit. Do you hear Paul writing to the Philippians?

> Yet indeed I also count all things loss for the excellence of the knowledge of Christ Jesus my Lord, for whom I have suffered the loss of all things, and count them as rubbish, that I may gain Christ and be found in Him, not having my own righteousness, which is from the law, but that which is through faith in Christ, the righteousness which is from God by

> faith; that I may know Him and the power of His resurrection, and the fellowship of His sufferings, being conformed to His death, if, by any means, I may attain to the resurrection from the dead. Not that I have already attained, or am already perfected; but I press on, that I may lay hold of that for which Christ Jesus has also laid hold of me. Brethren, I do not count myself to have apprehended; but one thing I do, forgetting those things which are behind and reaching forward to those things which are ahead, I press toward the goal for the prize of the upward call of God in Christ Jesus. (Philippians 3:8–14)

Paul writes this as a man who is already in the way. Christ has laid hold upon him. But he does not consider himself to have already attained or to be already perfected. Because he is in the way, he presses along the way, reaching forward to those things which are ahead. This is the spirit that presses on to lay hold of that for which Christ laid hold of us, to obtain the prize of the upward call of God in Christ Jesus. This is to follow the Christ who, through his servants, urges us to walk just as he walked:

> Therefore we also, since we are surrounded by so great a cloud of witnesses, let us lay aside every weight, and the sin which so easily ensnares us, and let us run with endurance the race that is set before us, looking unto Jesus, the author and finisher of our faith, who for the joy that was set before Him endured the cross, despising the shame, and has sat down at the right hand of the throne of God. For consider Him who endured such hostility from sinners against Himself, lest you become weary and

discouraged in your souls. You have not yet resisted to
bloodshed, striving against sin. (Hebrews 12:1–4)

When we consider him, we ourselves ought to be stirred to follow
in his footsteps. Do we consider him, and so run? 'Therefore
strengthen the hands which hang down, and the feeble knees, and
make straight paths for your feet, so that what is lame may not be
dislocated, but rather be healed' (Hebrews 12:12–13). No man can
march to Jerusalem with feeble knees! Unless we take up our cross
and follow him we cannot be his disciples. This is the whole
pattern of a Christian life. Such a spirit must govern and impel us
in the matter of salvation as a whole, colouring the whole scheme
of life.

But it cannot remain at a general level. This is not just how
salvation is advanced in the whole, but also how it progresses in its
individual elements. There are distinctive parts that fit together to
make up a holistically godly life. To each one of us a path is
appointed. To each one a calling is given. Every Christian has
particular duties set out as men and women of God, as church
members, as family members, as part of our earthly communities.
This spirit must characterise every part of life, it must give form and
force to particular duties and acts of holy obedience. It is this spirit
that should animate us in acts apparently mundane and potentially
extraordinary, serving God and seeking the good of others.

There is in us and among us too much aimless drifting rather
than fixing our eye upon God-appointed goals. Do you know
where you are going? Do you know what you are trying to
accomplish as a saint? Do you have any well-formed sense of who
God has made you and where God has put you and for what
reasons and purposes?

There is in us and among us too much cowardly avoiding rather than courageous obeying. Too many Christians turn in circles while bending over backwards to avoid anything that seems too difficult. Such a posture turns us into spiritual grotesques. 'Anything for an easy life!' Anything to avoid tension, confrontation, cost, hardship, discomfort of any kind.

There is in us and among us too much casual shifting rather than forceful progress. Even when it is plain to us where we should go and what we have to overcome, we shuffle rather than stride. We are content to stumble along rather than to forge ahead. Again, this is not a matter simply of doing more. It is a matter of doing the right things in the right way.

But why? Why make such efforts? Why pay such a price? Why cultivate such a costly spirit? Because the Son of God served us and saved us by giving his life as a ransom for the lives of his people. If Christ has so died for us, can we not so live for him? If that does not stir us, if that does not compel us, we have to go back to the cross and gaze again and learn afresh until we are ready to follow where he leads. It is what we will try to do particularly in the next chapter of this book as we seek to know him and better to serve him.

But how? If your life is characterised by aimless drifting and cowardly avoiding and casual moving, where will the change come? How do we get out of such a meandering path? This Christlike spirit grows under scriptural instruction, by spiritual illumination and thanks to spiritual invigoration. You must get back to your Bible to find the way you must go, the life you can expect, and the blessings you can anticipate. You need the ministry of God's Word and the fellowship of God's people to guide you and to encourage you—you have helps that Christ himself did not have as he trod the winepress alone (Is 63:3). But, essentially, you live this life relying on the same resources as our Saviour. The Spirit of Christ will supply us and sustain us, just as he did him, as we turn to the same Bible for instruction and direction, and press along the way our Master went and a disciple follows.

In the coming pages we will meditate upon this spirit as it was manifest in Christ particularly in the matter of his death and our salvation, and then turn to consider how we can cultivate a Christlike spirit of holy determination for ourselves. Even now, determine before God to live your life as a Christlike man or woman. Fix your eyes on the goals that God has appointed for you, count the cost of the way as God lays it before you, pursue your path to the end, for the glory of God, the good of others, and the joy of your own souls.

SALVATION SECURED

Now they were on the road, going up to Jerusalem,
and Jesus was going before them; and they were
amazed. And as they followed they were afraid. Then
He took the twelve aside again and began to tell them
the things that would happen to Him: 'Behold, we
are going up to Jerusalem, and the Son of Man will
be betrayed to the chief priests and to the scribes; and
they will condemn Him to death and deliver Him to
the Gentiles; and they will mock Him, and scourge
Him, and spit on Him, and kill Him. And the third
day He will rise again.' (Mark 10:32–34)

As we have seen, these verses reveal something of the spirit in
which Christ marched up to Jerusalem. They give us a glimpse of his
holy determination and righteous resolve. Reading the Scriptures of
God as a man illuminated and invigorated by the Holy Spirit, Christ
grasped his goal, counted the cost and pursued his path. In doing so,
he secured salvation for each one of his people. It ought to
characterise us as we seek the salvation he secured and live out that
salvation as a whole and in its individual elements.

However, we ought to pause to ponder this spirit that was
characteristic of our Lord's endeavour. We should dwell upon this
further, not least because it lies at the very heart of every true good

that we truly enjoy. If we are, and wish to be, strong-souled children of God, Christ must be increasingly precious to us, and Calvary must be a familiar place to us. All our spiritual health and happiness rests not just upon the fact of Christ's life, death and resurrection, but upon our grasp of it. We must see, know, trust and love the Christ who died on the cross, in all the horror and the splendour of his atoning work. For this reason, the saint never wearies of desiring and pursuing a better grasp upon Christ. How could we weary of dwelling upon him in whom lies all our hope and joy?

But it is also worth our while to pause and ponder here because, when it comes to cultivating this spirit for ourselves, we are exhorted to 'consider him' (Hebrews 12:3). It is all too easy for the children of God to lose our own determination and resolution, to become faint and to falter. It is by considering him who loved us and gave himself for us that such a spirit is restored and stirred. More particularly, how is it that Christ worked out who he was and what he did from the Scriptures? How did he find and follow that way? Humbly seeking more detailed answers to such questions should give us an insight into the very heart of Christ, and so provide us with comfort and instruction. When we see the Captain of our salvation standing fast and stretching forward, then we ourselves, by his Spirit within us, ought to be moved both to a proper adoration and a proper emulation of him.

Let us, then, take this passage as a case study in holy determination, a portrait of righteous resolution, a demonstration of what it means to be a servant of God. From whom could we more accurately learn than from *the* Servant of God, seeing how he traced out and embraced his duty?

THE LORD JESUS GRASPED HIS IDENTITY

Our Lord describes himself here as 'the Son of Man.' He refers to himself in the third person. This is his idea of who he is as he carries out the work he has been given to do. Christ's sense of his own identity is a profound and wonderful study. We cannot entirely trace out his self-awareness and self-disclosure, but we must stop and consider it more carefully. Even so we are merely dipping a toe into the waters of an unfathomable ocean of wonder. So, how did the Lord Jesus know who he was? Why does he call himself 'the Son of Man?' Where did he derive this understanding of himself?

Think first of the details of his conception and his birth. We know that he was conceived in the womb of a virgin, a woman who had never known an intimate physical relationship with any man. We know that he was born in Bethlehem. We know that angelic messengers having already informed Mary his mother and Joseph his foster father of what would happen, more angels appeared on the hills around Jerusalem to sing the praises of a saving God. The shepherds on the hills around the town, to whom those angelic hosts appeared, came down to Bethlehem and saw the infant Saviour and made widely known all that had happened to him. Wise men also came from the East and bowed down before the child, worshipping him. Joseph was further warned in a dream of the threat from Herod to the life of Jesus, and so spent time in Egypt, in accordance with the promise to Hosea that God would call his Son out of Egypt. In due course he returned to Nazareth.

Can we really imagine that a perfect child, growing in sense and understanding as God intended, does not hear such things from his mother and foster-father and begin to draw the threads together? We know that these were things his mother kept in her heart and pondered (Luke 2:19, 51). Did she perhaps tell some of them to her son at some point? Who knows what conversations he had with his foster father, Joseph, as he grew? By the time he was twelve years old he knew enough to tell Joseph and Mary that he ought to be about his heavenly Father's business (Luke 2:49). Nevertheless, he remained subject to them even as he increased yet more in wisdom and in stature, and in favour with God and men (Luke 2:52). What profound meditations he must have made and penetrating conclusions he must have reached as he traced out the lines of revelation with regard to his own identity!

Add to that the declarations and affirmations of John the Baptist. 'Behold,' says the greatest mere man who has ever lived, pointing at Jesus of Nazareth, 'the Lamb of God who takes away the sin of the world!' (John 1:29). Include not only the words of the man who baptised him, but the staggering testimonies from heaven itself associated with his baptism: John said that Jesus Christ was the one upon whom the Spirit descended and remained (John 1:32-34) so that he had the Spirit without measure (John 3:34). He did so because the heavens had opened and the Spirit had come down in appearance like a dove, and a voice was heard from on high, saying, 'This is my beloved Son, in whom I am well pleased!' (Matthew 3:17).

How much information there is, even from his earliest youth, both in terms of the events that happen to him and the necessary connections made with the Scriptures written about him. As Jesus the learning child, Jesus the growing boy, Jesus the developing youth, Jesus the maturing man, reads his Old Testament, he is looking at the information that he finds there, and he is reading concrete detail about the unmistakable events of his own life, written down centuries before they came to pass! By the time he begins his public ministry, he is both very willing and well able to sit down before those who knew him from infancy, and read from the scroll of the prophet Isaiah, and declare without embarrassment or uncertainty, with direct reference to himself, 'Today this Scripture is fulfilled in your hearing' (Luke 4:21).

This is the one who is now calling himself 'the Son of Man.' This is much more than a declaration that he knows himself to be fully human, or is in some way a kind of Everyman. In identifying himself as the Son of Man, our Jesus is probably drawing his language from Daniel 7:13: 'I was watching in the night visions, and behold, One like the Son of Man, coming with the clouds of heaven! He came to the Ancient of Days, and they brought Him near before Him.' We might also consider the description of Psalm 80:17: 'Let Your hand be upon the man of Your right hand, upon the son of man whom You made strong for Yourself.' Here is a man from heaven, one who is both divine and human, one who is humble among the arrogance of the bestial kings of earth, one who submits to the authority of the Ancient of Days, one invested by God Almighty with regal power and glory in his distinctive role. This is the Son of Man who came into the world (Mark 10:45). This is the name, the title, that the Lord Jesus deliberately takes for himself. He knows that he is the eternal Son of God and he asserts his identity as the man who comes from heaven in a unique way. He is not simply made, but he who is from of old entered his creation in order to accomplish his saving purposes.

In other words, the Lord Jesus is fully aware of his inherent authority, dignity and majesty as the eternal Son of God who became man in order to serve his heavenly Father and redeem his needy people. He knows who he is! He deliberately takes to himself a title—the Son of Man—that communicates with great purity and clarity his role as Messiah. His sense of who he is contrary to all those who would have confused and abused his calling. It is a sense that rises above all carnal and crass notions, and it is the sense that is foremost in his mind as he strides up to Jerusalem.

THE LORD JESUS EMBRACED HIS ACTIVITY

And so the Lord Jesus speaks: 'The Son of Man will be...'

Will be what? What happens to the Son of Man when he arrives in Jerusalem? If you begin to get some sense of his identity from the Scriptures, how do you expect that sentence to finish? How do you want it to finish? What will happen to this kingly one, true God and true man, as he travels to the place in which God has made himself known?

Will he be exalted on high? Enthroned over all? Praised above every name? Glorified as worthy? It is where you expect to go. It is where you ought to go. But—no! It is not where Christ goes. He will be a celestial sufferer and appointed substitute at the very centre of God's sacrificial system, God's redemptive purposes. The Lord Christ knew that the Son of Man was also the Servant of God described so eloquently and portrayed so painfully by Isaiah and others. He is going to Jerusalem to undergo the sufferings depicted in the words of the prophets. Why? Because Jerusalem was the place where the nation gathered for the sacrifice of Passover. Because Jerusalem was the place of the temple with all its depictions of eternal and heavenly realities and all its shadowy acts of worship pointing to the one great and finished sacrifice. Because Jerusalem was the place appointed by God for judicial process to be carried out (Deuteronomy 17:8-13). Jerusalem was the place where a prophet ought to be tried: 'it cannot be that a prophet should perish outside of Jerusalem' (Luke 13:33). His calling as a prophet will be tested and established in this place. It was the place which the King must enter, the King who is just and has salvation, 'lowly and riding on a donkey, a colt, the foal of a donkey' (Zechariah 9:9), and so Jesus must go in humble state into the holy city. It is the place the inhabitants of which must look on the one whom they pierced (Zechariah 12:10), and so Jesus must die there. And so the Son of Man goes up to Jerusalem.

But not only is the *place* set out, so too are the *pains*. The sufferings set before him are fearful in their intensity, foreshadowed through the Scriptures. In Psalm 2, the nations rage and the Jews plot, the kings setting themselves and the rulers taking counsel 'against the Lord and against His Anointed, saying, 'Let us break their bonds in pieces and cast away their cords from us' (v1–3). So Christ is handed over to the Gentiles by the Jewish authorities.

Antagonism gives way to aggression: 'But I am a worm, and no man; a reproach of men, and despised by the people. All those who see Me ridicule Me; they shoot out the lip, they shake the head, saying, 'He trusted in the Lord, let Him rescue Him; let Him deliver Him, since He delights in Him!'' (Ps 22:6–8). Eventually he reaches the very point of shameful death:

> I am poured out like water,
> And all My bones are out of joint;
> My heart is like wax;
> It has melted within Me.
> My strength is dried up like a potsherd,
> And My tongue clings to My jaws;
> You have brought Me to the dust of death.
> For dogs have surrounded Me;
> The congregation of the wicked has enclosed Me.
> They pierced My hands and My feet;
> I can count all My bones.
> They look and stare at Me.

They divide My garments among them,

And for My clothing they cast lots. (Psalm 22:14–18)

This is 'the stone which the builders rejected' (Psalm 118:22). In so suffering and dying, he gave his back to those who struck him, and his cheeks to those who plucked out the beard; he did not hide his face from shame and spitting (Isaiah 50:6). This is the innocent one of whom Isaiah writes in language of graphic immediacy:

> Surely He has borne our griefs and carried our sorrows; yet we esteemed Him stricken, smitten by God, and afflicted. But He was wounded for our transgressions, He was bruised for our iniquities; the chastisement for our peace was upon Him, and by His stripes we are healed. All we like sheep have gone astray; we have turned, every one, to his own way; and the Lord has laid on Him the iniquity of us all. He was oppressed and He was afflicted, yet He opened not His mouth; He was led as a lamb to the slaughter, and as a sheep before its shearers is silent, so He opened not His mouth. He was taken from prison and from judgment, and who will declare His generation? For He was cut off from the land of the living; for the transgressions of My people He was stricken. And they made His grave with the wicked —but with the rich at His death, because He had done no violence, nor was any deceit in His mouth. Yet it pleased the Lord to bruise Him; He has put Him to grief. (Isaiah 53:4–10)

He was betrayed by his own familiar friend for the wage of 'thirty pieces of silver'—'that princely price' (Zechariah 11:12–13)! We cannot help but see, as we read with Spirit-opened eyes, the experience of our Lord marked out. It is why we can preach the full-orbed gospel just as readily from the pages of the Old Testament as we can from the New, for all of the Scriptures speak of him who is the very centre and substance of the gospel. And we are reading from the very same book as the Lord Jesus did as he worked out what he was called to be and to do. From the first book of the Bible, Genesis, with its first promise of the Seed of the woman who would crush the head of the serpent, and in the act of triumph would himself receive that awful wound to the heel, it is impossible to avoid the theme. Christ had a Bible that told him that 'Messiah shall be cut off, but not for Himself' (Daniel 9:26). This is the unequivocal, reiterated testimony of Scripture. It prefigures with painful and undeniable accuracy the particular sufferings of the Lord Jesus Christ. Over and over again it describes and defines the precise nature of his life with its sufferings and sorrows and his death with its agonies and miseries. All the types and shadows of a suffering Saviour point to the cross, and that Saviour knew that the culmination and consummation of all those types and shadows required that he lay down his life. When John the Baptist saw Jesus coming toward him, that son of a priest cried out, 'Behold! The Lamb of God who takes away the sin of the world!' (John 1:29). He saw in Jesus of Nazareth the final, definitive sacrifice who would redeem his people from their sins by dying in their place. He saw the fulfilment of God's saving purposes.

That thread of substitution runs through the Bible's testimony about Christ's pains: this is suffering for others, what is sometimes called 'penal substitutionary atonement.' This is a sweet mouthful! It means, simply, a price paid to take away sins through the death of another in the place of those who deserve the punishment which he receives instead of them. Remember, *he* has borne *our* griefs and carried *our* sorrows; yet we esteemed *him* stricken, smitten by God, and afflicted. But *he* was wounded for *our* transgressions, *he* was bruised for *our* iniquities; the chastisement for *our* peace was upon *him*, and by *his* stripes *we* are healed. The language of certainty and necessity is used of this transaction: 'And He began to teach them that the Son of Man *must* suffer many things, and be rejected by the elders and chief priests and scribes, and be killed, and after three days rise again' (Mark 8:31); or, 'how is it written concerning the Son of Man, that He *must* suffer many things and be treated with contempt?' (Mark 9:12). It will happen! It must happen! The place must be Jerusalem. The pains must be precisely those predicted and required of Messiah. The purpose of salvation cannot be accomplished without this. Christ knows the holiness of his heavenly Father and the horror of sin. He knows these things far better, far more accurately and deeply, than any of us can. He went up to Jerusalem to suffer and to die for others. When we properly grasp the great gulf between God in his holiness and the sinner in his wretchedness, we ask less, 'Why is this necessary?' and more, 'What else could have both demonstrated and satisfied divine justice?' Nothing but the blood of the Lamb of God could close this breach. What scheme could mortal man dare to conceive or suggest to bring sinners back to God? What else but this great redemptive act could secure our life? All other provisions were shadows, insubstantial pointers to this great and effectual sacrifice.

THE LORD JESUS ANTICIPATED HIS VICTORY

It is difficult to know where to draw these lines. Jesus Christ told his disciples that on the third day the Son of Man will rise again. We must remember, even if we cannot grasp as we might wish, that the fact that these sufferings must occur does not in any way remove the responsibility of those who imposed them upon the

Redeemer. The fact that the victory is assured does not in any way lessen the determination of the man who procured it nor the agony he underwent as he did so. These truths are not tangled with each other but woven together.

Yet again, the confidence of Christ was grounded in Scripture. He embraced the cross in anticipation of the crown. Very often, the same passages which portray his suffering also underline his victory, for the cross and the crown were bound together. This is not the conviction or the language of someone who simply shrugs his shoulders and vaguely assures himself or others, 'Don't worry, it will probably all work out OK in the end.' This is a man who is determined to follow his course. There is no salvation otherwise. He does it, because it is written of him in God's book. This is faith in operation! This is confident expectation! This is the note of our own heavenly hope! We have the same confidence! The Bible speaks about our future. Those things are sure, because this is the word of God. Christ marches upon Jerusalem with faith to follow the path appointed in the Scriptures, through suffering to glory.

So in Psalm 2, though the nations of the world and the nation of Israel turns against him, the Lord still says to him, 'You are My Son, today I have begotten You' (Psalm 2:7). He can know that 'You will not leave my soul in Sheol, nor will You allow Your Holy One to see corruption' (Psalm 16:10). The wrestling of Psalm 22 gives way to settled and joyful assurance: 'You have answered Me. I will declare Your name to My brethren; in the midst of the assembly I will praise You. You who fear the Lord, praise Him! All you descendants of Jacob, glorify Him, and fear Him, all you offspring of Israel! For He has not despised nor abhorred the affliction of the afflicted; nor has He hidden His face from Him; but when He cried to Him, He heard' (Psalm 22:21–24). 'These are the enemies gathered around me; these the sufferings washing over me.' Nevertheless, says Christ, 'You, O God, you have spoken certainties to me, and I hang all my hopes and expectations upon you!'

David knew that the Lord would say to his Lord, 'Sit at My right hand, till I make Your enemies Your footstool,' testifying that the Lord would send the rod of Messiah's strength out of Zion, and that he would rule in the midst of his enemies (Psalm 110:1–2). Christ knew that this was spoken of him. That stone which the builders rejected would become the chief cornerstone (Psalm 118:22). Isaiah's declaration of a bruised man, put to grief by the Lord, gives way to an affirmation of triumph even in the very face of death:

> When You make His soul an offering for sin, He shall see His seed, He shall prolong His days, and the pleasure of the Lord shall prosper in His hand. He shall see the labor of His soul, and be satisfied. By His knowledge My righteous Servant shall justify many, for He shall bear their iniquities. Therefore I will divide Him a portion with the great, and He shall divide the spoil with the strong, because He poured out His soul unto death, and He was numbered with the transgressors, and He bore the sin of many, and made intercession for the transgressors (Isaiah 53:10–12).

The language of awful death gives way to the language of triumphant life! The same prophet declared good news on God's behalf: 'Incline your ear, and come to Me. Hear, and your soul shall live; and I will make an everlasting covenant with you—the sure mercies of David' (Isaiah 55:3). Hosea told us that 'after two days He will revive us; on the third day He will raise us up, that we may live in His sight' (Hosea 6:2)—God is everything he declared he was to Israel: 'Now see that I, even I, am He, and there is no God besides Me; I kill and I make alive; I wound and I heal; nor is there any who can deliver from My hand' (Deuteronomy 32:39).

These are the very notes which the apostle Paul picks up in Romans 1:4 when he testifies that Jesus of Nazareth was declared to be the Son of God with power according to the Spirit of holiness, by the resurrection from the dead. These are the threads he weaves together in Antioch when he preaches the good news of salvation:

> Now when they had fulfilled all that was written concerning Him, they took Him down from the tree and laid Him in a tomb. But God raised Him from the dead. He was seen for many days by those who came up with Him from Galilee to Jerusalem, who are His witnesses to the people. And we declare to you glad tidings—that promise which was made to the fathers. God has fulfilled this for us their children, in that He has raised up Jesus. As it is also written in the second Psalm: 'You are My Son, Today I have begotten You.' And that He raised Him from the dead, no more to return to corruption, He has spoken thus: 'I will give you the sure mercies of David.' Therefore He also says in another Psalm: 'You will not allow Your Holy One to see corruption.' For David, after he had served his own generation by the will of God, fell asleep, was buried with his fathers, and saw corruption; but He whom God raised up saw no corruption. (Acts 13:29–37)

The resurrection is the very demonstration of Christ's victory over sin and death and hell. It is the event which underlines with overwhelming reality and unassailable finality the fact that the sufferings of the Saviour accomplished their purpose. When he dies, the deep cry of his soul echoes around Jerusalem and bounces off its walls, from the place outside the gate: 'It is finished!' That cry resounds three days later around the chamber of his empty tomb: it is finished indeed! This resurrection is God's stamp of approval— the demonstration of the sufficiency and security of the work that God the Son has done. Christ on the cross cries, 'It is finished!' Christ coming forth from the tomb testifies that it has indeed been accepted. And now, the Son of God incarnate, the glorious Son of Man, having accomplished his task, has been exalted to the highest place, his not just by right of nature but now also by right of conquest. He has triumphed!

But it is relatively easy to read that back into the Scriptures after the event, comparatively easy to accept the resurrection after the resurrection has taken place. Christ went to his death with faith in these words written in the Bible. He offered himself up in the agonies of the cross because he knew that this was the way in which he would deliver his people and that he would be satisfied and glorified in consequence. It is one thing to acknowledge it. What faith it must have taken to accomplish it!

And all this the Lord Jesus embraced and pursued in order that he might secure, through this salvation, the glory and exaltation of his God and Father. This redemption is a demonstration of the glorious perfections of God himself. Christ could tell his disciples that the one who had seen him had seen the Father (Jn 14:9). Where do we see God in his justice? God in his power? God in his mercy? God in his wisdom? These attributes shine in all his works, but they are never more clear, more bright, more harmoniously and gloriously interwoven, than in the death of Jesus Christ for his people. What is God like? If you are asked that question, you might point to Calvary and say, 'He is like *that*. He is like *him*.'

Had the glory of God been Christ's whole and sole reason for what he did it would have been reason enough. But this is a demonstration of those divine glories which also actually establishes a blessing for men and women. Christ did all this not to make salvation merely possible. He did not suffer to make salvation even probable. He died and rose to save his people from their sins once and for all. We are delivered by his death and resurrection. The price is paid. You, believer, are safe in him.

And, in glorifying God and blessing men, Christ was pressing toward joy, the joy of his own soul in the accomplishment of these purposes. It was this which carried him through the agonies of Calvary with his eye on the glory which was to come. There was joy for the Servant in anticipation. He believed that he would see the labour of his soul and be satisfied. He was persuaded that by his knowledge he would, as God's righteous Servant, justify many, bearing their iniquities. As a consequence of this finished work, his heavenly Father would divide him a portion with the great and grant that he might divide the spoil with the strong (Isaiah 53:11–12). This Jesus is 'the author and finisher of our faith, who for the joy that was set before Him endured the cross, despising the shame, and has sat down at the right hand of the throne of God' (Hebrews 12:2). There was joy in the fulfilment of his work. He is now rejoicing in this accomplishments. He is dividing the spoil! He is looking back from the other side of the grave, and he is gathering in all the fruit of his labours.

So we should go on 'looking unto Jesus' (Hebrews 12:2). We should be entrusting our undying souls to this Saviour who died but rose again on the third day. Whoever believes in this Jesus—in the Son of Man who died and rose—is living in the light and the power of this victory. As we begin to consider what this same spirit looks like in us, we must never lose sight of the fact that Christ is

Saviour before he is Exemplar. His death is not merely a moral demonstration but a mighty redemption. His example would mock us if not for his atonement to deliver us. Unless and until his death has conquered your death and his life has secured your life, your service will be at best a shell of religion.

Is this why we hear and read and are not changed? When the Scriptures are believed, and salvation is enjoyed, and the Saviour known, then do we begin to be volunteers in the day of his power (Psalm 110:3). We cannot serve him until he has shown himself to us as the one who came not to be served, but to serve, and to give his life a ransom for many. When we grasp this Saviour and his salvation, and are grasped by him, we can begin to live out what we have received. All the preacher's urgings and the writer's exhortations fall to the ground unless we are captured by, depending on, and enraptured by this Jesus, this Saviour, this Son of Man who died for our sins in our place and rose for our justification. May God grant us such hearts, and all that flows from them!

GRASPING THE GOALS

We have considered Christ's holy determination in principle and in practice. We have seen his convictions and his actions as he secures salvation for his people. He reveals a single-minded devotion, determination and dedication with regard to his purpose: he will accomplish the work which his heavenly Father has given him to carry out. In so saving us, the Lord Jesus calls us into the same way, to walk as disciples in the footsteps of our Master. We have seen our Redeemer and our Master grasping the goals, counting the cost, and pursuing the path involved in such a life of obedience. We need to understand that we are called to follow our Master in such a course. We are saved in order that we might serve and glorify our Lord. Our labours are to be the means of securing blessing for others. In such a life we will be close to God and so full of joy and peace. We are instructed by the same Scriptures and enlivened by the same Spirit.

Such a spirit of holy determination which we see in the Lord Christ is a corrective to the aimless and vague Christianity which we see so often in our own day. It exposes the lazy and casual Christianity into which we too easily slip. Properly embraced, this attitude with its consequent actions is an antidote to lethargic and casual service of our God. It is the spirit that has characterised and galvanised the saints of the Bible and God's servants through history.

45

Think of a man like Joshua, of whom the Lord asks, 'Have I not commanded you? Be strong and of good courage; do not be afraid, nor be dismayed, for the Lord your God is with you wherever you go' (Joshua 1:9). Joshua has both the divine directive and the promise, and is therefore called to get up and get on with what the Lord has called him to do. What of Nehemiah? He has the promises of God, as did Daniel before him, who could discern from the Word of God that the period spoken of by Jeremiah the prophet concerning the desolations of Jerusalem were coming to an end (Daniel 9.2-3). So Nehemiah goes up with the people to rebuild Jerusalem and re-establish the worship of God in a restored temple, and he presses on in the face of discouragements, obstacles and enemies. We could think of Moses, of the judges, of David. We could consider Paul, Peter or John, or countless other New Testament believers who gave their all in the cause of Christ. We could think of early believers like Athanasius, of whom it was said that he stood against the world, sometimes seeming to be the one man who held to the truth of the Scriptures concerning God as triune and the deity of Christ the Son, though all others seemed to follow error. Or there is aged Polycarp, called to curse the Christ whom he believed or to die, who replied, 'Eighty-six years I have been his servant, yet in all this time he has not so much as once hurt me. How then may I blaspheme my King and sovereign Lord, who has thus saved [or preserved] me?'[2] We could roll on through the centuries, picking out men like Wycliffe, and Hus, and Luther, and Calvin, and Zwingli, and Bucer. We could consider Latimer and Ridley and Cranmer. We might consider Whitefield's labours, or the efforts of Carey who urged himself and others to expect great things from God and attempt great things for God. There is

[2] *Foxe's Book of Martyrs*, ed. A. Clarke (London: Ward, Lock and Co., n.d.), 20.

Spurgeon, especially during the Downgrade Controversy, holding fast to the Word of God and its plain sense when academic liberalism was threatening to swamp the churches. I hope you know names like these, together with the convictions and actions specifically associated with them. Yes, each of these were saved sinners, and therefore imperfect men and women. Nevertheless, there is a common thread holding them together: following after Christ, they were marked by holy determination. They knew what they were called to be and do, they were often painfully conscious of the cost of that call, and they embraced the call nonetheless. This is the spirit that we need to cultivate if we are to serve God in our generation as they did in theirs. We need men and women with faces like a flint. It is the spirit that the Word of God calls us to model for those who will follow after us.

We have already seen something of it in the person of our Lord Jesus. To study it out more completely and to learn it more specifically we will turn to Psalm 119. The whole of this psalm testifies to this attitude. Each stanza breathes an air of dependence on God and determination to obey, never apart from each other, but intertwined with each other. It gives us a window into a heart committed to the glory of God and zealous to hold to that way. We will focus on a few verses which exemplify the outlook we are considering:

> I have chosen the way of truth;
> Your judgments I have laid before me.
> I cling to Your testimonies;
> O Lord, do not put me to shame!
> I will run the course of Your commandments,
> For You shall enlarge my heart. (Psalm 119:30–32)

Looking at these verses will reveal three vital strands of a Christlike spirit of holy determination: grasping the goals, counting the cost,

47

and pursuing the path. We will consider and illustrate each of these elements in turn as we seek the glory of God, the blessing of others, and the joy that such a life brings to our own souls. We begin with the words of Psalm 119:30: 'I have chosen the way of truth; Your judgments I have laid before me.'

A PRINCIPLED COMMITMENT

The man of God says, 'I have chosen the way of truth.' This is an intelligent, deliberate and settled decision on his part. It is not a mere acknowledgement that the truth has some passing influence upon him. It is not a matter of casual preference, as when you might choose this bar of chocolate over that one when looking for a treat. You could choose from any one of a number of options and it would make very little difference, except for a temporary effect upon the tastebuds.

This man's selection is not a concession to a casual acquaintance with the Word of God or the pressure of some particular companion or circumstance, likely to change as soon as his company or situation changes. He has thought this through in the light of divine truth and has chosen accordingly. It is a positive and personal embrace. Faith does not make assumptions and faith is not blind. It is properly discerning, and it lays ahold of what it discerns reasonably and fiercely. That is true of the faith that comes to and clings to Christ, and the faith that goes on following the Christ.

This, then, did not happen by accident. It is a definite choice and not a dozy chance. The man who stumbles into the way of truth is just as likely to stumble straight back out again. The man who merely happens to walk into a right road, almost accidentally, might be quickly driven or drawn out of it. In contrast, this man has reached a positive conclusion that this way of truth is for him.

This choice is also personal: it has not, in that sense, been chosen for him. Of course, we acknowledge that the child of God is a child of God by God's choice. But in calling him to God in Christ, the Spirit of God has freed and enlivened his heart. So liberated, he makes his decision. The mind of this man has been enlightened by the Spirit of God. He has already been praying in the course of this psalm for instruction and understanding, for vigour of soul in the place of declension and dullness. God is at work in him to give him insight into the truth and conviction resulting from it. Nothing has been imposed upon him. In the Scriptures, there are men like Joash, who promised and even accomplished so much while Jehoiada the priest was his counsellor, but who so quickly departed from the ways of the Lord when Jehoiada died and other advisors took his place (2 Chronicles 24). It seems that Joash was never wedded to the truth; he could be swayed into it, but also swayed out of it. His heart was never committed to the way of righteousness. It is why, in the Book of Proverbs, the father who is instructing his son pleads, 'My son, give me your heart, and let your eyes observe my ways' (Proverbs 23:26). The father wants the son to make a positive, personal choice, and to learn accordingly. You must calculate the cost and then embrace the right path.

Moses, to whom all the wealth and wonder of Egypt was held out, chose 'rather to suffer affliction with the people of God than to enjoy the passing pleasures of sin' (Hebrews 11:25). He looked at the options, weighed up the issues, and then made an intelligent, deliberate and settled decision. Like Moses before him, the psalmist has embraced the way of truth with a full sense of what is at stake, and he has no desire or intention to waver from his principled commitment to the truth. In the words of Matthew Henry, 'The choosing Christian is likely to be the steady Christian.'[3] Having laid hold, he holds fast.

A RIGHTEOUS CHOICE

This is also a moral choice. He has already pleaded with God to remove from him the way of lying (v29), turning his back once and for all on error and falsehood. In its place he chooses truth, he takes God's judgments. The first phrase—'I have chosen your truth'— points to Scripture as the rule of conduct from which the believer will not deviate. It is a determination faithfully to follow the truth of him who is Faithful and True (Revelation 19:11). He chooses reality as it is seen through the lens of God's revelation.

The second phrase—'your judgments I have laid before me'— identifies the divine decisions and determinations as the reference point in ordering every aspect of our faith and every step of our lives. This believer has a clear awareness of the twisted alternatives to God's truth. There is a plainly implied consciousness of these seductions and persecutions which need to be actively resisted if we are not to be tossed to and fro and carried about by every wind of doctrine (Ephesians 4:14). It is why he soon cries out, 'I cling to your testimonies!' (v31). Having laid hold of the truth, he is determined not to let it go at any cost. To use New Testament language, this is the spirit that readily and willingly chooses and embraces Christ as the way, the truth, and the life, taking him over and in the face of all else and any others. Like Peter, such a one

---

[3] Matthew Henry, *Matthew Henry's Commentary on the Whole Bible: Complete and Unabridged in One Volume* (Peabody: Hendrickson, 1994), 916.

asks, 'Lord, to whom shall we go? You have the words of eternal life' (Jn 6:68).

℣

A STEADFAST CONVICTION

Note that these governing principles—the decisions and determinations of the Lord God himself—do not float vaguely somewhere in the distant background of this man's life. They are before his eyes. Walk through any big city these days and you will see people moving around with their eyes fixed on their smartphones, relying absolutely on the directions they are hearing or watching or reading for every step they take. The old commentator Paul Bayne says simply, 'Men that mean to travel the right way will lay before them a map.'[4]

This is not the foolish man who is persuaded that he always knows his way regardless of the possession or, indeed, the use of a map, much to the frustration of all those travelling with him. Rather, this is the attitude of God's servant. Having chosen this way of truth, he holds God's judgments continually before him as his standard for and guide through life. God's directives are the object of his sincere affection and his cheerful obedience. He delights in the revelation of God, and he is not afraid to express his high esteem of it. But he does not merely appreciate it, he actually does it. Like a child learning to write, he must keep the outline of God's word always before him and trace over the letters in his life.

---

[4] Quoted by C. H. Spurgeon, *The Treasury of David: Psalms 111-119*, vol. 5 (London; Edinburgh; New York: Marshall Brothers, n.d.), 204.

Spurgeon tells us that 'the commands of God must be set before us as the mark to aim at, the model to work by, the road to walk in.'[5]

Is this your pattern of life, believer? Is this the way in which you go through the world? This man of God provides us with a Christlike model. Do you have any godly goals toward which you are striving in a spirit of holy determination? What desires and designs are you cultivating for your character and convictions as a means of bringing glory to God and blessing to others? What are you striving toward?

If you saw someone wandering about or driving in circles, would you not conclude that they did not know where they were going? They will remain lost until they work out which route they need to take and begin to take it. Too many Christians are wandering aimlessly or turning in less-than-saintly circles. They do not know what they are trying to accomplish. They do not have any idea of which is the next turn, the right turn. How do we expect to get anywhere in the Christian life if we do not know where we are going? As we have seen, this is the spirit and the rule that must condition our pursuit of salvation, both in its broad scope and in its distinctive or separate elements.

To do this, like Christ before us, we must choose the way of truth and set God's judgments before us. Survey your life at this moment, and answer this question: 'Are you any closer?' If you have any sense, your likely answer will be another question: 'To what?' And that is precisely the point! We cannot tell if we are making progress unless we know where we are heading. How can you go further, and know that you are going further, if you have no idea of where you are trying to reach? We need to set the judgments of God before us! Our faith and life must be formed and

[5] C. H. Spurgeon, *The Treasury of David: Psalms 111-119*, vol. 5 (London; Edinburgh; New York: Marshall Brothers, n.d.), 192.

informed by the Word of God and pursued in dependence on the Holy Spirit: the truth of God must govern our goals. That does not mean that we are looking for a proof text for every thought, word and deed, as if we cannot move without an explicit directive in clear words from the Bible. Not every act of Christian obedience is a response to an absolute and absolutely plain directive from Scripture. Neither does dependence on the Holy Spirit mean being driven about mindlessly by the whims of our own souls, as if we are receiving a constant stream of new revelation, making wild or wilful decisions and claiming that we are operating under the immediate guidance of the Lord God.

This means a mind illuminated by the Spirit of God, studying the Word of God prayerfully and carefully, sensitive to the Spirit's operations upon our hearts, in order that we may know the way of truth, in order to choose it, holding the judgments of God before us. It means that we are increasingly conditioned by the Word of God in all its fullness and force as the Holy Spirit impresses it upon our hearts.

We obey the *precepts* of Scripture, positively and negatively, where they speak plainly. If the Word of God says, absolutely, 'Do this,' or 'Do not do that,' I willingly and carefully obey it. Plain commands and prohibitions like those of Ephesians 5:1-4, for example, are binding on our souls, and need simply to be understood and followed, not discussed and massaged until they become more palatable to the sinful soul or acceptable to the modern world:

> Therefore be imitators of God as dear children. And walk in love, as Christ also has loved us and given Himself for us, an offering and a sacrifice to God for a sweet-smelling aroma. But fornication and all uncleanness or covetousness, let it not even be named

among you, as is fitting for saints; neither filthiness, nor foolish talking, nor coarse jesting, which are not fitting, but rather giving of thanks.

We apply the *principles* of Scripture as they are clearly laid out, extracting and applying general rules of righteousness to our specific circumstances. For example, we may not have Roman-style slaves in the way the wealthier saints in Colosse had. Nevertheless, Paul's commands to them—'Masters, give your bondservants what is just and fair, knowing that you also have a Master in heaven' (Colossians 4:1)—can be readily applied to the more modern relationships of the employer and employee in almost any culture. It means something about the management, working conditions and salaries of the staff who are under the employer's care. It scarcely needs pointing out that the preceding verses of Colossians 3:22-25, with their vigorous call to do what we do heartily, as to the Lord and not to men, has evident application in our lazy and distracted generation.

We imitate the *patterns* of Scripture, as they demonstrate holiness. There are godly men and women whose righteous deeds we should emulate, and whose errors of judgment and sinful behaviour we should learn to avoid at all costs. We can learn from Moses what it is to be meek, and be warned by Moses not to break out in anger. Abraham calls us to a life of faith, even by the demonstration of his willingness to sacrifice his own promised son with the sure confidence that the Lord can raise him from the dead (Romans 4.16-22). Abraham also warns us against lapses into faithlessness, against taking matters into our own hands, such as with Hagar or when he felt threatened by his marriage to a beautiful woman when living among fierce men. We have Job's patience, Daniel's righteousness, Paul's confidence, to be models for us. We embrace those patterns, as they guide us in godliness.

God's book is enough to tell us how to live. Its truth makes us wise for salvation through faith which is in Christ Jesus (2 Timothy 3:15). It will show the unbeliever the Saviour who delivers from sin and calls to righteousness. It holds out a man who died that you might live. All who desire such blessings must find the blessed Redeemer as he is portrayed in the pages of Scripture. But, furthermore, all Scripture is given by inspiration of God, and is profitable for doctrine, for reproof, for correction, for instruction in righteousness, that the man of God may be complete, thoroughly equipped for every good work (2 Timothy 3:16–17). The whole revelation of God provides all that is necessary for maturity as Christians. From its pages we derive our marching orders, both the more generic directions and targets that govern the lives of all Christians, and the more specific encouragements and directives that answer to our very specific situations and individual circumstances.

We might note in passing that pastors and preachers have twin responsibilities in this regard. You might know the saying, 'Give a man a fish and you feed him for a day; teach a man to fish and you feed him for life.' Very often pastors get into the habit—perhaps encouraged by lazy Christians—of doing all the fishing and cooking for God's people. They simply put the food before the saints in order that believers might eat. Now, in some sense, that is part and parcel of his duty: his calling involves the finding and preparing of spiritual food for the people of God (Ephesians 4:11 *ff.*). The elders of the church ought to be preachers and teachers of the truth. However, the true pastor also wants those whom he serves to learn to fish for themselves, so that they are able to stand, having been edified by the ministry of the Word. He equips the saints to live before God with their own convictions in action. Christian maturity cannot involve calling a pastor every time there is a decision demanding more than a modicum of sanctified common sense. Pastors not only feed with fish, they teach to fish. There are many moments when Christians need to stand for themselves on the Word of God, to demonstrate their personal commitment to the Scriptures. Pastors cannot always hold God's people by the hand. When other Christians are not present and pastors are not available, and the moment of trial or temptation comes, that is when it will be proved whether or not *you* have chosen the way of life, whether or not *you* have set God's judgments before you. Those moments at which it is far easier to go with the flow, drift with the current, follow the herd, are the moments at which Christian conviction is revealed as real or otherwise.

Goals worth grasping

What sorts of things are we talking about? Let me offer some illustrative examples in quite developed and ripe language. The sentences are long but careful, intended to give in one dose a fairly complete idea of particular obedience. While in each case there are more specific elements which we would need to work out for ourselves, would you nevertheless agree with the following as appropriate goals of the more generic kind for which the saints will need a face like a flint?

As individuals, such goals might have to do with private devotion, the pursuit of godliness, and local church membership. Christians should be pursuing the consistent and profitable pursuit of substantial communion with the Lord through a habit of systematic, sustained and prayerful exposure and response to the word of God in a spirit of devotion. We should make a definite, determined, repentant assault on particular sins married to a principled and vigorous cultivation of the corresponding graces with a view to Christlike maturity. We should embrace a willing, determined, habitual commitment to and investment in the life of the local church in accordance with our gifts and graces.

In our families, we might think of family worship, godly marriages, and gracious and righteous parenting with a proper response from obedient children. Christians should commit to a regular pattern of appropriate, affectionate, lively, deliberate, submissive exposure of the whole family to the whole counsel of God. We should pursue a genuine, grace-soaked and gospel-grounded relationship between husband and wife demonstrating the one-flesh reality of the union while embracing the distinctive roles. We should cultivate from every side of the relationships involved a thorough, cheerful and genuine spirit of ready obedience from children to the God-given authority of parents.

As churches, what of our love for the saints, and engagement in worship, and cheerful confidence in God? Surely we should seek a transparent, earnest, principled affection which intentionally, actively and sacrificially cultivates sincere fellowship with and seeks the well-being of the whole body and its individual members. We should develop a humble but hopeful appetite for corporate worship as the highest expression of the church's identity in which we eagerly seek God's face together and anticipate a blessing from him. We should pursue a sustained and healthy expectation that God's appointed means will accomplish God's appointed ends among us, through us, and around us.

I hope that every reader of this book would give hearty agreement to such goals. My friend, if you are reading this and you do not, or you simply do not care, or if you find your gorge rising against such oppressive requirements, if you feel that these are burdens unbearable and unreasonable, then you need to ask serious questions about your spiritual health and even your spiritual identity. These things are not really much more or less than the time-honoured expectations of healthy children of God.

But we should go further. Even if we do offer hearty agreement, do we know why? Could we establish these principles and practices? Could you open your Bible and show where you get the language and the substance of such commitments? Could we, at least in some measure, define, demonstrate and defend these things from the Word of God? Could we develop their pursuit, making clear how and why we would go about them? More pointedly, how do these particular things apply particularly to you—your life, your virtues and your vices, your family, the church to which you belong? You may dislike sin. You may wish you were free from it. But what are you doing to fight it, in yourself and in others? If your pastor asked you about your present battles with sin and for righteousness, you should be able to answer him. If you are not sure, could that be why you so rarely win those battles, if you are even fighting them? Are we thinking about the best ways to minister the gospel to our families, so that we are consistently exposing the whole family to the saving truth in a lively and engaging way, showing that Dad and Mum are themselves in subjection to the God who speaks in the Scripture? Do you know what a child is, according to the Bible? Can you explain what are the particular opportunities, dangers, blessings and needs of a child? That will make a difference to how you teach and train, what you expect and allow, and how much and how soon you allow your growing son or daughter to take particular responsibilities and pursue particular paths. Are you a parent who recognises your own God-given authority in the home which you govern in gracious but principled love?

Perhaps you could not answer these questions, and others like them, off the cuff. If not, are you learning, bit by bit, at least to open your Bible, seek out the right portions and passages, and begin to construct something of a biblical rationale for the way you live and why you live like that?

Without intelligent and principled commitment, without a righteous choice and a steadfast conviction, you will more quickly be swept aside. You will become like the pragmatic Israelites of Judges 1 who found the driving out of the godless nations a bit too much like hard work, and decided that they would live alongside of them instead. Too many of us make peace with our sins, and compromise on the pursuit of righteousness. We will lose our distinctiveness as the people of God unless we choose the way of truth and lay God's judgments before us. Paul spoke to the church in Rome about obeying from the heart that form of doctrine to which they had been delivered (Romans 6:17). This pattern of teaching was not just delivered to them, but they had been delivered to it! It kept them as much as they kept it.

Are these things so woven into our spiritual DNA that they have become part of us? In themselves, these matters that we have identified constitute quite basic biblical Christianity. They are the sorts of things that ought quickly to become normal for new Christians. Perhaps the reason why so many of us struggle with the sweep and the detail of these basics is that we have never got these things into our spiritual systems.

We ought to be like the Bereans, who received readily all the things that they received from their credible and proven teachers of truth, and then searched the Scriptures daily to find out whether or not these things were so (Acts 17:11). The Bereans both eagerly ate the fish that they were served and worked hard at their own fishing! We too must be people of the Book, embracing and obeying God's Word.

Christian men have a particular responsibility here, especially those who are also husbands and fathers, to be genuine leaders in the church and in their homes, setting the pace and maintaining the pace, and helping others to do the same. Men who wholeheartedly follow Christ become true standard-bearers and standard-setters. Those who hear the preaching of God's Word should be working its substance into their own souls and reproducing it in their lives. We should determine to hear and to do the truth.

But let us not imagine that this spirit and service is restricted to men only. How often has the church of Christ been held together (humanly speaking) by the testimony of a few faithful women? I know of a number of churches in the UK where the work was sustained, sometimes for several years, by a very few but very faithful women of God. Who has not seen women of principled courage holding the line in their homes while their wavering husbands—to their shame—bluster and fudge? Furthermore, when a married woman positively pursues her own full-orbed godly femininity, she does not undermine or compete with her husband, but enables him more easily and readily to be the man that God has called him to be.

Folding or fighting?

So what is the problem? Why are we so slow to identify, accept and grasp biblically-grounded goals? For some of us, the problem is simply that we will not. We are not interested. We make excuses. We evade the force of God's Word as it is explained and applied. In fact, we get into a habit of evasion. We become accustomed to choosing the path of short-term ease. If we do not take ourselves in hand, we shall remain aimless saints and spiritual pygmies. I say, to my great personal grief, that many of the people who have drifted in and then out of the church which I serve are those who have resisted all encouragements and exhortations to embrace basic biblical responsibilities. They often like the idea of the spiritual product, but they have no appetite for the spiritual processes which bring about that end. They have never chosen the way of truth.

For others of us, the problem is a culpable *cannot*—I mean, we say we cannot, though we should be able to! We have never bothered making the principled commitments, pursuing the righteous choices, and cultivating the steadfast convictions that will support us in the pursuit of basic godliness. We then find ourselves too busy, or too weary, or too… anything but getting on with the pursuit of godliness! If we do not have time to set God's judgments before us, then we need to clear out some junk from our lives. If we do not have the spiritual energy to choose the way of truth, then we ought to stop wasting that energy on frivolities. Are there not, perhaps, even some otherwise legitimate demands that we might need to put to one side in order to concentrate on greater priorities? Too often, despite being offered encouragements and support, help and counsel, we keep sliding away. We never bother carving out the time or investing the energy that these holy duties demand. Eternity is at stake, but our present resources seem too precious to invest in it.

For others still, it is a genuine difficulty. You would say, 'This is the kind of man I want to be. This is the kind of woman I aspire to be.' There is real desire, real appetite, but they have never had the models or instruction that they need. You may not have been converted very long, but you are eager to follow Christ. Often, such friends—once given help—will quickly outstrip those who have countless privileges but never bother using them. Perhaps they are younger Christians who are coming in from difficult circumstances and now need to be taught to obey all the things that

Christ has commanded (Matthew 28:18-20). Such believers need to be not criticised and dismissed, but helped, encouraged, taught and instructed. Those who have been privileged to grow under healthy instruction must be ready to take the new disciples under their wing and teach them to obey our Lord and Saviour at every point, confident of his presence with them. For all such hungry saints, the pastors must be diligent in preparing fine fishy meals, as well as equipping them to search the Scriptures for themselves.

What do those Scriptures principally teach? According to the Shorter Catechism—no bad place to start for those who want to grasp some godly goals—the Scriptures principally teach what man is to believe concerning God, and what duty God requires of man. So we must get back to our Bibles. We must bind our consciences and direct our lives according to the Word of God. A bound conscience is a right and proper thing when it is bound to God's revelation. We need the conviction of a Luther, who at that critical moment of his pilgrimage, confronted with all the splendour of Roman might, said, 'My conscience is captive to the Word of God.' He had chosen the way of truth. He had laid God's judgments before him.

We need to grasp our goals as God defines them for us, to get their contours and colours established in the light of divine revelation. We must choose the way of truth. We must hold God's judgments before our eyes. We are saved for such a life. We have many battles to fight in pursuing these goals, and we shall turn to consider those in a moment. However, unless we know where we are travelling, and why and how we should make our journey, we shall never get anywhere, let alone arrive at our destination. Let us no longer be wandering Christians and aimless saints, but walk as we are called.

❧

COUNTING THE COST

We are considering the soul of the man or woman who has been captured and enraptured by Jesus Christ as Lord and Saviour. We are looking at those who have set out as true disciples of Jesus along the road to glory. We have seen Christ's own example in winning our salvation. Now we are considering our response to that purchased blessing as we work out, with fear and trembling, that salvation won by Christ for us and worked by God in us, through the Holy Spirit (Philippians 2:12-13).

We have observed that the child of God must establish spiritually healthy and scripturally sound goals, both with regard to their grand scope and minute detail. We gave some time-honoured but fairly basic examples of the areas of life in which we would need to do just that. Have you done so? Perhaps you have slipped straight into this chapter from the last, and have not paused to consider the pressure of those things? Will you do so now? I encourage you to pause for a moment. Engage in a little deliberate self-examination. Consider more carefully and personally the areas and issues in which you need to choose the way of truth and set God's judgments before you. Do not ignore Christ's example. Do not despise the scriptural model. Do not despise my counsel. The preaching and teaching of God's Word is so that we may prove both hearers and doers of the truth. We need to choose ways of truth in which we have not yet learned to walk. We need to lay God's judgments before us for particular areas of life. Have you made your determinations?

It may be that you have already grasped some of your goals. You have thought through the Word of God at some of the particular points at which it touches your particular life, applying its irresistible pressure to conform us to Christ. But it may also be that you need to sift through your faith and your life, acknowledging those areas where you are aimless or have become careless, identifying those points at which you need to step up. Beware, especially, the tendency to isolate and exempt certain aspects of life from this process. It is too easy to give the impression of comprehensive obedience while actually reserving some crevices of the heart in which sins might fester. In any case, it would be good for each of us to pause and to settle at least two or three areas in which we will determine where we are going and how we expect to get there and what that will take. If we are resistant even to the idea of doing so, of course neither I nor anyone else can make you do this, but I will mourn that so many saints go on ignoring Christ's example, Scripture's pattern, and pastors' counsels. We must get to grips with these things if we are to grow in grace.

But what next? What happens once we have grasped our goals? Perhaps we have sought to do this in the past and we have realised very quickly just how tough is this process. Once we have set our standards and grasped our goals from the Word of God, it sometimes takes only an hour or two, perhaps a few days, to realise the enormity of the task before us. We perhaps start off at a good pace, but soon hit barriers and lose our momentum. It should not be a surprise to us. When the Lord Jesus set out to save his people, he met with enemies and obstacles at every turn. If we follow the Master, we should expect the same.

We do need to choose the way of truth and to set God's judgments before us. But we need to do something more than that. We must go on with the author of Psalm 119 to confess and to cry, 'I cling to Your testimonies; O Lord, do not put me to shame!' (v31). The path of righteousness is not a red carpet strewn with rose petals, but a rocky road with its thorns and thistles, potholes and gullies. It is a difficult way, though straight and true and upward. We must learn to face and to overcome the obstacles and the enemies that face us. We need to make a realistic assessment and to embrace a righteous response.

If I want you to feed on fish and to learn to fish, here I would also encourage you to keep on both eating and fishing! We have quoted Matthew Henry, who said that 'the choosing Christian is likely to be the steady Christian;' however, he went on to warn that 'those that are Christians by chance tack about if the wind turn.'[6] It is this danger of changing course when things go against us which we must now address. It is because the way is hard that we cry out to God to help us as we seek to hold fast.

⁂

THE MATTER OF THE CHRISTIAN'S CONCERN

As in the previous verse, the primary concern of the believer is God's revelation. He has spoken of 'the way of truth' and the judgments of God. Now he speaks of 'your testimonies' and then, in turn, 'your commandments.' Although there are subtle shades of meaning here, these are all near-synonyms for the revelation by which God makes himself and his will known. It is God's path of righteousness, the way of communion with him, made plain.

This man has discerned and chosen divine truth, and he is still taken up with it. It delights and excites him, it holds and upholds him. It is not a passing interest or a temporary fad, but a deep and abiding attachment. Consider how he esteems the Word of God as

---

[6] Matthew Henry, *Matthew Henry's Commentary on the Whole Bible: Complete and Unabridged in One Volume* (Peabody: Hendrickson, 1994), 916.

it expressed here in Psalm 119: it gives him joy (v14); he delights in it (v16, 24); he ponders it (v23); he considers it good (v39); it brings him salvation and life (v41, 50); he loves it (v47-48); he hopes in it (v49); it is precious to him (v72, 127, 162); he is confident that it is right (v75); it comforts him (v76); it is settled and sure (v89); it is sweet (v103); it gives light (v105); it is lasting (v111); it is pure (v140). He could hardly esteem it more highly. By it he has learned to love God, hate sin and seek righteousness. The Word of God guides him, just as it should us if we know 'the Holy Scriptures, which are able to make you wise for salvation through faith which is in Christ Jesus.' Furthermore, 'all Scripture is given by inspiration of God, and is profitable for doctrine, for reproof, for correction, for instruction in righteousness, that the man of God may be complete, thoroughly equipped for every good work' (2 Timothy 3:15–17).

If these are reasons for us to choose the Word of God and to hold fast to his judgments in the first place, then those are equally reasons why we should continue to cling to those testimonies in the face of whatever pressures would carry us from them. Have you made this choice? Have you so esteemed the truth of God? What is your attitude to and esteem of the Word of God? When did you last open it? Do you value it more than your necessary food? Is it sweeter to you than honey and more precious than much fine gold? Have you found life in Christ as he held forth in the Book of God? Have you been made by the Spirit to see your sin, God's grace, and Christ's salvation as you study the Bible? Have you found your course mapped out for you in the Scriptures? Is it precious to you because in it your God has opened his mouth and spoken to you all that you need to live to the praise of his glory?

A Christian's great concern is the truth of God. The Lord's gracious revelation of himself to us as creatures and as sinners, and then—because of his further grace toward us—as his servants, is a matter of abiding interest and deep affection for every true believer.

THE VIGOUR OF THE CHRISTIAN'S CONVICTION

'I cling to your testimonies.' These are tones of force and fervour! 'There is no word expressing closer adherence.'[7] You cannot speak of a fiercer attachment. This man is holding fast with all his might! It is the language of fierce loyalty to and complete absorption in the object. This is the firmest of resolutions in the midst of trials and troubles and temptations, the most ardent grasp on something precious against all pressures and difficulties. It involves a battle to hold fast, the kind of battle of which the apostle spoke: 'For I delight in the law of God according to the inward man. But I see another law in my members, warring against the law of my mind, and bringing me into captivity to the law of sin which is in my members. O wretched man that I am! Who will deliver me from this body of death? I thank God—through Jesus Christ our Lord! So then, with the mind I myself serve the law of God, but with the flesh the law of sin' (Romans 7:22–25). He feels the tension, and fights for truth.

Faith grips truth; love embraces truth; hope holds to truth. This Christian is a human limpet: he is glued to the rock of God's word by a near-unbreakable bond. Apparently, British engineers have concluded that limpets' teeth consist of the strongest biological material ever tested. I usually carry with me a small pocket knife, but it now has some chips in the blade. That is because I have used it to try to flip limpets off rocks along the sea shore. The trick is to

---

7 William Plumer, *Psalms* (Edinburgh: Banner of Truth, 1975), 1034.

slide the knife ever so gently under the edge of the shell and then to flip it off before the limpet can react. But it is the speed and strength of the reaction which is impressive. The moment the limpet discerns the least force prying it away from the rock, it snaps down hard, sufficiently fast and firm to leave chips in the steel of my knife blade. The stronger the force applied to get it off the rock, the more fiercely it clings to the rock.

So it is with the man of God. He is not a chameleon who changes colour to match his surroundings. He is one of God's colour guards who holds up the banner of his Lord in the midst of battle. He is not a twig swirled about on whatever current happens to be strongest. He is a vessel anchored in the midst of the storm. The more wind and tide press, the more deeply the anchor is embedded in the sea bed. He shows the spirit which Barnabas encouraged in Antioch, who—when he came and had seen the grace of God—'was glad, and encouraged them all that with purpose of heart they should continue with the Lord' (Acts 11:23).

Why such vigour? Why such fierce attachment? Why such fortitude? Why is it necessary? Why do the Christians in Antioch need to be encouraged to cling to God and walk in his ways? Because of all the pressure on the believer to be and do otherwise! There are so many influences against the way of truth that only the man who clings fast to God's testimonies will hold. Like them, we face the same pressures and assaults, and need the same reminders and encouragements.

There is the danger of *drifting off* the way of truth—the challenge of *confusion*. This can take a number of forms. It might be ignorance, a simple lack of knowledge that allows one to wander from the way. It might be weariness, the weight that makes us look for the apparently easier option to the path of righteousness. It might be distraction, when something catches our attention and we begin to follow thoughtlessly after it, or something holds our attention and we wander into danger. Perhaps it is unbelief, in which we do not believe that the truth of God is clear enough, or that it is too clear, too cutting. It might be pride, confident that it knows a better way than the one God has laid out. Some lack examples of faithfulness, and so see little danger in trying another route. For some it may be denial, simply turning one's back upon what seems too hard. It might be excuse-making, when the path takes us away from something we favour or toward something we don't, and we would rather it were otherwise. It could be bad habits learned years before and ingrained over time, where we have never broken out of a pattern of foolishness. It might simply be laziness, that the upward path of righteousness is not smooth and grassy, but painful and rocky, though straight toward heaven. Confusion concerning the truth often leads to us drifting off the right way.

There is the danger of *being drawn off* the way of truth—the challenge of *seduction*. Again, what a variety of shapes this can take, but usually under the guise of pleasure. It might be worldliness of a general or specific kind, the desire to be like others and have what they have and live as they live. Things off the route to heaven look more pleasant than the things that are on it. Perhaps there are particular temptations to sin, particular enticements that lie off the righteous way. For some, it is the call of apparent peace, the offer of an easy life, the absence of strife and struggle. The false promise of rest takes many into a side road. Applause draws many aside as they seek the favour of men who pour scorn on the hard paths of truth. Such invitations are rarely to go too far off the path of truth, but it is far enough to no longer be on it. Some travellers want the esteem of men, they desire respect and respectability—perhaps the tip of the academy's hat or the appreciation of the wealthy. For others, it is simple pleasure: the straightforward offer of worldly delights which God does not and will not offer because they are tainted with sin. Seduction from the truth often leads to us being drawn off the right way.

There is the danger of *being driven off* the way of truth—the challenge of *persecution*. Once more, we find a kaleidoscopic array of troubles. Here, it is pain that threatens rather than pleasure which entices. Although desiring men's favour is really a function of fear, it is more explicit here: the threatenings of aggression, of disdain, even of personal assault. This often begins with words, the scorn and abuse that begins to stream toward those who do not bow to the world's way of thinking and feeling and doing. Our Lord warned us of this:

> If the world hates you, you know that it hated Me before it hated you. If you were of the world, the world would love its own. Yet because you are not of the world, but I chose you out of the world, therefore the world hates you. Remember the word that I said to you, 'A servant is not greater than his master.' If they persecuted Me, they will also persecute you. If they kept My word, they will keep yours also. But all these things they will do to you for My name's sake, because they do not know Him who sent Me. (John 15:18–21)

When the Christian turns his or her back on lewdness, lusts, drunkenness, revelries, drinking parties and abominable idolatries in whatever form, the world will 'think it strange that you do not run with them in the same flood of dissipation, speaking evil of you' (1 Peter 4:4). But it might not be so outwardly aggressive: for some it is the slow grind of stubborn resistance, the steady trickle of scorn or pressure from families or friends which gradually wears away their resolve. Just because it does not come with flame and blade does not make it gentle and soft. Persecution because of the truth often leads to us being driven off the right way.

The Word of God states and restates its warnings about confusion, seduction and persecution. If you walk alongside the Old Testament saints, you will find the same challenges. You will see Abraham and his beautiful wife, going to the land of Abimelech, Abraham acting in fear rather than faith. He loses sight of the fact that the Lord can protect him, and has promised to do so. You see Moses taking matters into his own hands and killing the Egyptian who was assaulting his Israelite brothers. You see David, relaxing on the roof of his house rather than labouring on the field of battle, and his eye wandering toward the bathing Bathsheba.

Drawn off, drifting off, driven off—this is the pattern of spiritual warfare in this world. The psalmist is aware of all these foul pressures and fearful possibilities. He is trying to cling to the Lord's testimonies, but he feels these forces pushing or pulling him away, and so he cries out to the Lord.

THE INTENSITY OF THE CHRISTIAN'S CRY

The believer cries out in the midst of his battle to hold fast to the truth, 'O Lord, do not put me to shame!' He knows that there will be reproach and opposition to his stance. He knows that he is in danger of stumbling in the way. Therefore he looks up to heaven. He is conscious of his own weakness and of God's strength, of his need and God's goodness. He knows that he cannot stand alone, but he knows too that if the Lord holds him up, then all will be well. He is sure that he will only be able to hold on to God's truth if the God of truth holds on to him, as when he calls out earlier, 'I will keep Your statutes; oh, do not forsake me utterly!' (Psalm 119:8). He is determined to hold fast to the truth of the Lord in the face of all provocations and persecutions, but he does so in dependence on the Lord. He is clinging to the same kind of promises that Joel spoke concerning the true God among his saints: 'I am the Lord your God and there is no other. My people shall never be put to shame' (Joel 2:27). This is, we might say, a prayer for vindication: the child of God prays that he would not be made ashamed of his choice and commitment. He pleads that he would not come to confusion and dismay as when a man is overthrown by his enemies, brought face to face with the emptiness of whatever he was hoping or boasting in.

Do you feel the depth of his desire? He says, 'Lord, I have chosen your truth, and I will hold to it in the face of all pressures— but do not leave me to myself, lest I shame myself, offend the saints, and dishonour your name. Let me live so as to prove the excellence of your testimonies, to show the beauty and sufficiency of your words, to demonstrate their substance and their sweetness, their truth and their hope. Keep me when I cannot keep myself. Let me not become dismayed and confused. Demonstrate in your own good time that I have chosen well, and am walking in the right course. Vindicate me as your servant, so that your own name might be vindicated in me!' Could it be that one reason why we fail to cling is because so often we do not bother to cry?

Does that desire resonate with you? Is it not something of the spirit of Martin Luther at the Diet of Worms? There he faced down the Roman Emperor and his courtiers and scholars, his soul convicted by the testimony of Holy Scripture, his conscience captive to the Word of God, neither willing nor able to recant, and so casting himself upon the mercies of God. He clings to God's testimonies, with the earnest desire that the Lord would not put him to shame.

We need such prayers in our hearts. It is not unusual for a Christian to hold fast, to cling to the Lord, and to find the pressure against him building. The intensity of the opposition develops, and —should he then release his grip—that pressure means that he is often driven faster and further than would have been the case had he simply folded like a wet rag at the first sign of difficulty. Remember Peter: he was a man who loved Jesus more than almost everyone else. He followed him when almost all others fled. He walked into real and pressing danger because he was committed to Christ. The pressure against him built. When he crumbled, he denied his Lord three times, even with oaths and curses, contesting all suggestions that he knew and was attached to the one who was loving him and about to lay down his life for him. Oh, how we need grace to endure!

If you are a member of a faithful church, your sins and bad example bring dishonour to Christ and his body. We have a name —a proper reputation—as the people of the living God. Our failure to cling to him brings shame to Christ's people and to the Lord God himself. If you have made known to friends, neighbours and colleagues that you are one of Christ's, what is the effect when you stumble or seem to be swept away? So what do you pray? 'Lord, prove again and again that this is your excellent word! Prove that all the spiritual substance and sweetness and sufficiency that my soul requires is found in your testimonies! Vindicate me as your servant, and vindicate yourself as my God!' Do not think you will stand, lest you fall.

Such words as these make me thankful for an honest Bible. When Satan speaks, he holds out the bait but hides the hook. When God speaks, he both points out the cross and holds out the crown. Our pathetic age takes these warnings and turns them into excuses. But such honesty is not intended to put us off but to set us up! It is a warning, that we might be equipped beforehand. It calls us to make our decisions in the hour of relative ease, that we might not make our excuses in the hour of real battle. The moment of crisis will not form your character; it will only reveal it. You will not become holy when trouble threatens if you have not been holy when peace governs. You must now choose truth and cling to God's testimonies, praying for heavenly grace. Reckon with the battle and prepare to fight it.

Fighting the good fight

In his masterly story of the life of a Christian pilgrim, John Bunyan shows us a man who is offered the opportunity to enter a glorious but well-guarded palace. From among those who long to be in the palace but who seem unwilling to press toward the prize, a man finally steps forth. He puts his name down to fight his way in despite the opposition. The prize lies beyond the mob and the gate, and so he prepares himself for the fight. He enters into a long and painful combat, in which he gives and receives many wounds. Eventually he cuts his way through those who stand between him and it, and so wins his way into blessing. He was warned; he was prepared; he was committed; he was battered; he was victorious. That must be our spirit, and it will surely be our experience. Have you put down your name? Are you determined to enter in to the glory? Are you ready to fight and bleed? We fix our eye on the prize, we count the cost of obtaining it, the battles that must be fought to win it, and then we set out to get it, clinging to the truth and calling on the Lord. So our Lord admonishes us that 'No one, having put his hand to the plow, and looking back, is fit for the kingdom of God' (Luke 9:62). He told those who believed that 'If you abide in My word, you are My disciples indeed' (John 8:31). His apostles warn us starkly that for some 'it would have been better for them not to have known the way of righteousness, than having known it, to turn from the holy commandment delivered to them' (2 Peter 2:21).

Put this into the context of those three areas we have previously considered—the matters of individual holiness, family godliness, church righteousness. Can you begin to see how you might be drifting, drawn or driven from the way of truth in these things?

You intend that pattern of private devotion, but the mornings are dark and cold, and seem to start very early. The bed is warm, and an extra few minutes of sleep never hurt anyone. Then there might be something vital that has been revealed on social media overnight, and that is worth checking. And then—a few minutes later—there is breakfast to prepare, the kids to rouse, and work to get to. Somehow it never quite happened.

There is some sin to battle, but it happens to be quite a pleasant old companion—you don't need to see so much of him, but you would be loath to lose him altogether. To be sure, we want to be holy… but not just yet. Or we effectively conclude that—despite the promises of God—there is a pattern of sin in our lives that has just become so much a part of our identity that it now lies beyond the need or possibility of its being cut out. We tell our husband or our wife or our friends that our arrogance, bitterness, pride, rudeness or selfishness are just the way we are, and they had better get used to it.

You are exhorted to invest in the life of the church, but it cuts into your leisure time, it demands energy, and some people might think you're getting a little fanatical. It is possible to have too high an expectation on what is, after all, a family day. We know churches where you don't *have* to go to church once on Sunday, let alone be expected to attend more than once. Surely we can slide in a light 'God slot' when it is convenient and then move on? Anyway, perhaps there's a sermon online that would mean that I can pretend I was 'kind of' at church without actually having to make the effort of going among God's people.

You would like to get into a habit of family worship, but there is something on the television, and you're not quite sure what the various members of the family are going to expect from you, not to mention that at least one of the kids has made it quite clear that they are not too interested. The mornings might work, but they're pretty full—especially with that idea of a private devotional time that I keep intending to get round to introducing. Besides, I don't know what it is meant to involve, what it ought to sound like. I don't know how to pitch it, so I will never start it.

Yes, you would like to be closer to your wife or husband, but there would be some specific sins to confess (and your pride would rather find another way around that) and some specific sacrifices to make, and—quite frankly—life is easier without them. Do you really expect me to tell my spouse that I have been wrong for the whole of our married life? Where would that leave us? I might have to confess arrogance, cruelty, carelessness. I might have to tell my wife that it is easier to dominate her than to love her. I might have to tell my husband that it is easier to manipulate him to than to submit to him. Besides, if we were to really make progress I would need to talk to my spouse… for, like, an hour… at least every month!

And, yes, your children should obey you, but they don't, and you are too scared of them righteously to establish and graciously to enforce your authority. After all, we cannot really expect our children to obey us, can we? Surely the way to win our children to

Christ is to ease off, to back away, to ensure that there are never any lines of righteousness drawn in the life of our family? Or you are inclined simply to go on making excuses for their sin? They are a little tired, that's why they are stabbing each other with sticks. I mean, they only rage against parental authority when their allergies are playing up, poor mites! Are your children always too tired, too hungry, too sick, too needy, ever to be expected to obey? Good job there is no sin in their hearts! Of course, any kind of discipline doesn't really work. (Are you quite sure, never actually having tried it?) Actually, you do not really trust God's means to accomplish God's ends.

You would, of course, prefer healthy and transparent fellowship in the church, but then you would have to stop pretending that everything in your life is just the way it should be. You must be the sorted-out woman, the great man. I might come storming from home, but I must be seen to come sweetly to church, with spiritual syrup pouring from my hypocritical lips. We do not want to open our homes, empty our wallets and our cupboards to fill the stomachs of fellow members. We do not wish to rebuke one another's sins, confess our sins one to another, and take time to build, maintain, or restore relationships of sturdy love.

You would love to get more out of corporate worship, but your life is so disordered that you are never likely to arrive anything less than late and frazzled. To prepare to be ready to worship God takes more effort than it seems to repay. To be honest, just being there is hard enough and pretty wearisome. You so rarely actually get anything out of it, you are not sure why you should bother.

You would be ready to expect great things from God, but you have no time to consider them, no intention of attempting anything in relation to them, and are, to be honest, a little fed up in waiting for them. So much for God's great and precious promises!

When have we ever seen anything that the Scriptures or the histories would like us to imagine are possible? We have done so much and accomplished so little. Perhaps we should try something… someone… somewhere else?

Do you hear the language of confusion, seduction and persecution? If you set your mind to be godly, you are in for a fight. Where you take a stand, battle must be joined. You will only endure as you cling to God's testimonies.

What, then, are we to do in the face of such challenges? Perhaps the first thing that we have to do is to repent and obtain forgiveness. Once we have repented of being out of the way, we ought to choose it—to get back in it and to press along it. Yes, there are providential hindrances. There are legitimate difficulties and real obstacles to overcome. But, too often, the problem lies in our hearts. We need to choose the way of truth, and then to cling to God's testimonies with all our might, crying that our attachment and commitment would vindicate God with regard both to his truth and your faith. Ask the Lord that you might not stumble and fall. Take up the whole armour of God, that you may be able to withstand in the evil day, and having done all, to stand (Ephesians 6:13). You might have to say with Job, 'Though He slay me, yet will I trust Him' (Job 13:15), and to remember God's promise and warning that 'those who honour Me I will honour, and those who despise Me shall be lightly esteemed' (1 Samuel 2:30). Pray then, that you might be one who honours God. Pray that though the world and the flesh and the devil might all rise against you at that very point, that God would uphold you, to prove his faithfulness to you.

To that end, consider again your Saviour. He set his face like a flint. He reckoned with all that lay before him, all that lay between him and the accomplishment of that salvation for his people upon which he fixed his gaze. He set off with the desire and expectation that the Lord would vindicate him in that choice and that pursuit. God did so by raising him up and declaring him to be the Son of God with power by the resurrection from the dead. Christ did not so live and die and rise that we would live at a low ebb, wavering and whining. He did it so that we should take up our cross and follow him. There will be confusion, seduction and persecution with which we must contend. But the choosing Christian, the clinging Christian, must keep to the way, and get back on the way when drifting, driven, or drawn off it. As we go, we pray to God that he would not put us to shame.

We may not gain a public vindication in our life on this earth. Our death might not seem to have much good or glory attached to it. But we are waiting for the day of resurrection, when we shall hear the Captain of our salvation say, 'Well done, good and faithful servant; you were faithful over a few things, I will make you ruler over many things. Enter into the joy of your lord' (Matthew 25:21, 23). We cling to his testimonies in the light of a coming day in which none of his people shall be put to shame.

PURSUING THE PATH

We must both depend on the accomplishments of Christ and follow the example of Christ. We must not separate those two elements of our experience. In all we do we rest on what he has done for us. Going in the way of the Lord, we are seeking to cultivate a face like a flint—a Christlike spirit of holy determination that fixes its eye on a scriptural goal, counts the cost, and assesses the obstacles that the Bible warns lie ahead, and then pushes on to achieve its prize. This is the example both set and followed by the Lord Jesus himself as he marched up to Jerusalem to lay down his life for his people. He told his disciples where he was going and he made plain what was going to happen. Yet, with vigour and determination, he strode up ahead of them (Mark 10:32-34). Our Lord pressed ahead to bring glory to God, blessing to mankind, and joy to his own soul. Will you do the same? If we have been following the thread of this short book, we know what we fight for, and are now like an army drawn up before a foe on what we know will shortly become a bloody battlefield. The question is, 'How will you fight?' How will we go into battle? We see the course and the finishing line. How will we run the race? The question must be answered in the spirit of Psalm 119:32: 'I will run the course of Your commandments, for You shall enlarge my heart.' Christ not only knew the psalmist's spirit. He exemplified that spirit. We must cultivate it for ourselves.

THE BELIEVER'S RESOLUTION

'I will run,' declares the child of God. This is the spirit of firm and vigorous determination. It goes beyond sincere aspiration. It is the language of resolute responsibility and unshakeable commitment and energetic intention. The psalmist reveals more about his desire to run than about his ability to run. It is possible for a child of God to the outward eye to be shambling, even crawling, but inwardly to be running with all one's might. You might know of the park runs that take place around the United Kingdom and further afield: a five kilometre course marked out for runners of all ages and abilities every Saturday morning in a local park. There are near-infants as well as senior citizens. There are skinny sprinters and lumpen shufflers. Some are clad in lycra, bouncing up and down at the starting point in anticipation of a fleet departure. Others look as if they were rolled out of bed and dragged to the park without quite realising what was happening. But when the run begins, all of them set off. All are trying to get around the course as quickly as they are able. They have different capacities, but they are usually marked by the same spirit. This is less about your natural brilliance and more about your learned resilience. This is about running with all the strength and speed that we possess.

Far too much of our language and attitude as Christians is essentially passive or, at best, casually conditional. We wait for favourable circumstances, we look for ifs and buts. We say, 'I hope... I'll try... maybe... perhaps... if this, then...' We wait until our children are older, the church is larger, the finances are healthier, the preaching is better... and the chances are that the moment for action never quite comes. That is not a spirit of righteous resolution! We offer excuses and suggest delays, finding reasons not to do anything. In effect, we refuse to run until the world tilts so as to ensure that we are simply coasting downhill. That does not happen!

What are the right circumstances for running? When the starting pistol sounds! Then we begin running and we run to the end. This is the spirit of Christ and his most eminent servants. There was nothing conditional about the obedience of Christ and his true disciples: 'Brethren, I do not count myself to have apprehended; but one thing I do, forgetting those things which are behind and reaching forward to those things which are ahead, I press toward the goal for the prize of the upward call of God in Christ Jesus' (Philippians 3:13–14). Even the world will tell you that the man without zeal and resolve accomplishes nothing. The singleminded achievers of this world are often those who say, in effect, 'I will run.' They are not waiting until things seem easy. They plan, they purpose, they pursue, they fight past obstacles. Why do worldlings strive for a fading crown while Christians play with an eternal one? Christians are too often guilty of flapping and faffing and fluttering when great things are at stake.

It is also an intelligent determination. The same man who just spoke of clinging to what he has chosen now declares an equally positive outlook. He knows that the race will not be easy to run. We might be content simply to reach the end of the race in one piece. But in the face of all the opposition this runner anticipates and experiences, he is intending to pick up speed, actually to raise his game. Running speaks of vigour, urgency, immediacy, zeal, even pleasure. There is a drive and intensity and energy that characterises his activity. He has chosen and so he engages with all his strength. If he is to run, the believer cannot afford to be hindered by ignorance, burdened by a carnal love for this passing world, shackled by doubts and unbelief, chained down by sins. The Christian needs to be an athlete honed for spiritual competition, a man determined—on the one hand—not to give an inch and—on the other hand—to gain a mile with every step. No coach of an international rugby team would welcome into the team a man who did not know how to cling to ground gained and to run forward to gain ground, and yet Christians allegedly pressing toward heaven seem too often to be coasting along in the vague expectation that progress will simply happen.

Remember this is less about your capacity and more about your attitude. What is your spirit? There are too many armchair Christians, too many casual Christians. Sitting saints are tragically common. Running Christians are rarer by far and precious indeed. How much we need such saints as these! Are you resolved to run or simply ready to watch?

THE BELIEVER'S DIRECTION

This is not aimless activity: 'I will run the course of your commandments; I will press on along that particular way.' The Christian is not a headless chicken, all rapidly diminishing energy and wild misdirection. The believer's activity is not a matter of heat without light, of zeal without purpose. How frustrating it can be to see kingdom investments that are essentially pointless because fundamentally directionless! If you have an energetic young dog which you take for a walk, the poor beast has generally run about three miles without even leaving the car park. Too many Christians show the same commendable eagerness without thoughtful intention.

But still less is this disobedient activity. The Proverbs are full of warnings about those whose energy is directed toward wickedness, quick to plot and quicker to pursue their schemes, hearts that devise wicked plans and feet that are swift in running to evil

(Proverbs 6:18). Diligence and resolve in a course of god*less*ness is a fearful matter. Such things are abominable to God. Too easily we invest our energies in things that are displeasing to the Lord. Even true believers can end up with their time and energy not just wasted but wickedly cast away in the pursuit of things that are not just unworthy of them, but positively harmful to them.

Neither is it hypocritical activity, the dressing up of carnal schemes in righteous garments. Absalom promised much diligence in seeking justice for the poor and needy of the land (2 Sam fuel 15:1-6), but it was all intended to turn the hearts of the people of Israel away from their rightful king. Let us be careful not to perform for applause and for the promoting of our own reputations. There are too many people who are happy to give the impression of diligent service in order to gain influence, but without right motives.

It is terrible to pursue wickedness. It is wasteful to run in circles. It is delightful to obey. There is nothing unChristian, nothing legalistic, about a spirit of cheerful obedience in the spirit of a son with regard to his father. The believer looks to run in accordance with God's commandments. This is precisely the way in which the Son of God went about his life. He opened his Bible. He studied the truth. Enlightened by the Spirit, he came to a rich and full understanding of his calling and all that was involved in it. The same Bible that called him to his work revealed the cost of that work. Nevertheless, he set out with the confidence that—in accordance with his promises—his heavenly Father would vindicate him.

So it is with the adopted sons of the Father. The child of God is first concerned for God's glory, for God's approval, for God's delight, and for all that flows from them. This is why the psalmist cries from the beginning, 'Open my eyes, that I may see wondrous things from Your law' (Psalm 119:18). He wants the Lord to show him those things that he needs to know and so do to bring praise and glory to his name. The choice is made; a stand has been taken; he will run the course set out by God's appointment. He desires the delight of his Father in heaven toward him, and the glory of God's name because of him. There is no exception in this declaration. There is no selection made of the commandments that coincide with constitutional inclinations or personal preferences. He does not simply play to his strengths and overlook those instructions that speak to his weaknesses and sins. He does not merely follow the way that might bring prominence or applause, and avoid the turns that carry him into quiet paths of unseen service. Without exception, he embraces the Lord's word. The Christian has no liberty to pick and choose how, where, when and under what circumstances he will obey God. God is God! He has spoken. If God calls you and me to some particular way of thinking, feeling, willing or doing, then that is our path. Our part is simply to run in the course of his commandments. There is no spiritual space in the Christian's life that we can lock away from the gaze and government of God Almighty. If purchased by the blood of Christ, we are to present our bodies as living sacrifices, holy, acceptable to God, which is neither more nor less than our reasonable service (Romans 12:1). Is that your determination and direction? That you will not simply run, but run in obedience, characterised by whole-souled and ardent desires to be and to do all that the Lord calls us to be and to do? This is not the point at which we respond, 'I don't feel like it!' This is the point at which we expect renewed reason to choose, renewed will to lead and affection readily to follow. Here is the spirit of universal obedience.

Is this, then, your spirit? With your eye upon the goal, with an awareness of all that opposes, do you press on with wholehearted and ardent desires to serve your Lord? This is, as we have said, the way to enter the kingdom and the way to advance in it. This is the way that we are to believe as sinners and to obey as sons. Do you cry out for this? Do you cry out under this? Do you feel overwhelmed by the demands? Does it seem to require strength you do not have over a distance you cannot run? What a mercy that the verse does not finish there!

THE BELIEVER'S EXPECTATION

You may now be saying, 'But I just don't have it in me!' Let us be honest: you don't. But there is no deficiency in God. He has strength which we lack, wisdom we do not have. Such desires and determinations as these were implanted in us and embraced by us, and now they turn us outside of ourselves. They bring us—in submissive dependence—to the feet of our Saviour, our every faculty thoroughly subject to God himself. The root of such a spirit lies in God's mercies toward us. He is long suffering, gracious, patient and mighty. It is because God is gracious toward those who trust in him that we have hope. It is not the best man who will run like this so much as the man who knows God best. These desires only spring to life when God has called us out of darkness into his marvellous light: it is God who enlarges our hearts! The initial and ongoing pursuit of God and godliness can never be separated from Christ's saving accomplishments.

You will notice that the key blessing here, the key concern, is in the realm of grace rather than gift. God does not turn us into super humans, stretching us into unusual shapes for the pursuit of excellence in a narrow field. Rather, he enlarges our hearts. God expands our inner faculties to employ our lives for his glory.

Extravagant gifts are worthless without glorious grace to enliven them. A shrivelled, constrained, self-centred heart will accomplish little. A heart released from confinement, a heart liberated from its shackles, a heart turned toward God in Christ—that is the heart from which a prompt and cheerful obedience will issue.

This is where our spiritual energy for the race derives: it flows to us from God in Christ. 'I am the vine, you are the branches,' says our Lord. 'He who abides in Me, and I in him, bears much fruit; for without Me you can do nothing' (John 15:5). Drawn into a living relationship with Christ, the bonds fall from our souls. Dwelling upon and meditating upon him, our hearts are enlarged. This is why we have looked so much at the accomplishments and example of our Lord Jesus Christ—because this is where our spirits are expanded, where our understanding is enlightened, our love stirred, our joy increased, our godly fear enhanced. This is why we need to go on looking to Jesus. A Christ-filled sermon, a Christ-rich book, a Christ-centred conversation, is a tool for heart-enlarging spiritual surgery. It enables us to run where before we might have shambled. When our hearts are expanded, when our understanding is enlightened, when our love is stirred, when our joy is increased, when our godly fear is enhanced, as we come to a greater knowledge of the glory of God as it shines in the face of Jesus Christ... then we move! When we see our Saviour, our response should be, 'O God, I will run the way of your commandments.' Then we ask with the apostle, 'Lord, what do You want me to do?' (Acts 9:6). What does Isaiah say when he sees the glory of the pre-incarnate Christ in the temple at Jerusalem and feels the cleansing effects of the sacrifices? 'Here am I! Send me' (Isaiah 6:8). So says the enlivened heart: 'Point me, and I will go! Direct me, and I shall run!'

By their fruits you shall know them. Grand claims to communion with God without growing graces are empty boasts.

Do you know some who claim precious times of private devotion, high and rich thoughts of God, perhaps even immediate heavenly blessings from the very Spirit of Christ? Wonderful claims indeed! But one basic way to determine whether or not such claims have any substance is by whether or not the life changes. When a Christian man has been in the presence of God in that way, he is marked afterward by a whole-souled obedience to God, a marked and growing holiness. If that is missing, the experience to which that man lays claim is not heart-enlarging communion with God. If it were so, the evidence would be plain in the life lived before God and men.

Is your heart confined and constrained? Where do we go with our shrivelled souls? We must take them back to Gethsemane, where we see the Saviour crushed to the dust of the earth that he made. We must watch him wrestle with the awful sin-bearing that he has undertaken. We must take our hearts to Gabbatha, to the Pavement where, having been given into the hands of the Romans to be beaten, spat upon, scorned and mocked, his own people bay for his blood. We must go up with our souls to Golgotha, to Calvary! We must watch as the Son of God, the Lamb of God, hangs on a cross of wood and dies that we might live. We must become familiar with those places. We must fix our eyes and our hearts on these things. We must look on the Jesus who strode up to Jerusalem with his face like a flint until we are ready to say, 'O my God! I will run the course of your commandments! You are worthy, for you have saved us! You have made us kings and priests to God!'

Then go to the throne of grace with all your feebleness, failings, frailties and follies, all your sin, all your aimlessness and carelessness, all your drifting and erring, all your wandering and listlessness, and repent of your sins, and call upon the Lord to enlarge your heart.

You need strength for speed; it is the heart set free that will run with endurance. When God has all your heart he will get all your life, as he takes up residence and makes your soul his temple.

Running the race

So are you running *properly*? Having chosen the way of truth, will you now cling to his testimonies and run the way of his commandments? You are in a fight, and you will make no progress without real and sustained effort. You are in a race. Now is not the moment for slouching, sitting, and relaxing but for sprinting, striving, and racing. When do you get a rest? When the race is over! When you have reached the finishing line. Until then, you must run like a man or woman who intends to win a crown that does not perish.

Are you running *accurately*? Our running is marked out in accordance with God's saving intentions. We are called to run in the lanes of holiness. We are to pursue the Lord's course, not our own. We press on, that we may lay hold of that for which Christ Jesus has laid hold of us (Philippians 3:12). Paul's fervent endeavours for Christ are governed by Christ's gracious dealings with Paul. The apostle was once a blasphemer, a persecutor, and an insolent man (1 Timothy 1:13), an opposer of truth and an oppressor of believers. And there he is, striding toward Damascus for wicked purposes, and a divine hand reaches forth and grasps Paul in order to set him apart for holy service. From being Christ's enemy he becomes Christ's servant. Paul knows why Christ grasped hold of him, what end the Lord had in mind, and he knows, too, that he himself does not yet have his hands on that prize. He runs toward that goal in the way that Christ has established.

Is that true of us with regard to the whole course of our life and its individual strands? In our private communion, our assault on sin, our investment in and engagement with the local church, with our friends and in our marriages and families, in our embrace of the needy, are we running this race? These things ought to grip our hearts and compel our efforts. Christ ran to save us; we now run to serve him. Our labours are determined by his will. We gave up our own carnal appetites and fallen habits the day we met Christ. Christian, you said, in effect, 'Lord, you know far better than I. You tell me where to go. You tell me what to do. You send me; you guide me. I will follow you.'

But are you also running *dependently*? You cannot run this race in your own strength. You must rest on divine power:

> He gives power to the weak, and to those who have
> no might He increases strength. Even the youths shall
> faint and be weary, and the young men shall utterly
> fall, but those who wait on the Lord shall renew their
> strength; They shall mount up with wings like eagles,
> they shall run and not be weary, they shall walk and
> not faint. (Isaiah 40:29–31)

We must anticipate and rely on divine strength and then run in the confidence that God will equip us, strengthen us and sustain us to reach our goal, just as he did with his own beloved Son, by his gracious Spirit. This can be and should be our expectation. The Lord has promised that he will never leave us nor forsake us. As Christ under the Spirit's guidance identified his calling, reckoned with its costliness, and ran its course, so too may we. So too must we, if we are to be faithful servants of our heavenly Master.

One step at a time

Go back again with me to our examples, our categories and instances of obedience. Do you have some hard yards to make in these and other matters? If you are a true child of God, that is certainly true. Not all of us must concentrate on the same issues to the same degree. We have different circumstances and face different demands, but we need the same spirit of holy endeavour, of holy determination. We all have work to do.

Perhaps you know what it is to sprint out of the chapel door on the Lord's day after the sermons, but to be crawling by the time you reach your car or your home. You might know what it is to read your Bible or some other book and to leap up ready for action, only to have that intent simply fritter away in the face of the immediate challenges that the desire for obedience brings. You may be already readying your reasons as to why I should lower my expectations for you, or why you might lower them for yourself. There may be some genuine and particular reasons why such expectations are hard to attain. But, let us be blunt: often this is simply making excuses. Some say, 'If only you knew what my [life/ wife/husband/children/circumstances/other problem] was like...' It is true. I don't know. Some of it I could probably guess, but I do not know the details of your life. But that is not the point.

The question with us should not be, should never be, 'Is this hard?' The question we really need to ask is this: 'Is this right?' Is it the Lord's commandment, a divine judgment, a heavenly testimony? If it is right, Christ has died that he might have you and that you might give your all in the matter, your best, for his joy and yours, for your blessing and the blessing of others through your endeavours. You may even be crawling in your body, but running in your heart, and the Lord will smile upon you and sustain you.

Let us by all means mourn over our smallness of heart, but let us not make our weakness an excuse for laziness and low attainments. Make it rather the reason why you pray for grace and strength! 'My heart is shrivelled! O Lord, enlarge my heart! My heart is shackled!

Show me Christ in such a way as to set me free to run! Make me live to your name.' Consider who set you on your feet, who raised you up, who marked out your way, who calls you to run, who strengthens you along the path, who is waiting at the end:

> Therefore we also, since we are surrounded by so great a cloud of witnesses, let us lay aside every weight, and the sin which so easily ensnares us, and let us run with endurance the race that is set before us, looking unto Jesus, the author and finisher of our faith, who for the joy that was set before Him endured the cross, despising the shame, and has sat down at the right hand of the throne of God. For consider Him who endured such hostility from sinners against Himself, lest you become weary and discouraged in your souls... Therefore strengthen the hands which hang down, and the feeble knees, and make straight paths for your feet, so that what is lame may not be dislocated, but rather be healed. (Hebrews 12:1-3, 12-13)

Do you ever pray that you would be a hearer and a doer of God's Word (James 1:22-25)? It is right to do so, but here is the opportunity to prove it. If we pray like this without any intention of living like this we will bring judgment on our heads. Will you evade, resent, drift, stagnate, recede? Will you recast God's commandments to make them a little more attainable or a little more palatable? Or will you face and embrace, choose and pursue, the course that Christ has marked out for his people? We are called to press on with a face like a flint and a heart aflame. May God enlarge your heart and make you a Christlike runner, characterised by holy determination, growing in the grace and knowledge of our

Lord, and bringing glory to God, blessing to others, and joy to your own soul.

O God, our God,
There is no one like you in heaven or on earth.
You alone are God, to be believed, adored, and obeyed.
You gave your only-begotten Son that sinners might not die
but live,
and declare the works of the Lord.

But my life has not been what it should.
My soul has clung to the dust;
Revive me according to your word.

Forgive me, gracious God,
for my cowardice, laziness, hypocrisy and disobedience.
Merciful Father, enlarge my heart,
and the hearts of all your people,
that we might run in the way that you have appointed.

O God, we make no vague statements of desire;
we offer no shoddy and insubstantial aspirations.

As your believing people, we make it our holy resolution:
'I will run the course of your commandments.'

Our gracious Saviour, we have your pattern before us.
Gracious Spirit, you are with us to strengthen us and
illuminate us.
Gracious Father, you have blessed us and given us grace.

We ask then, O God Most High, that our service of you
might be our constant and increasing delight;
that you would be glorified,
that we would be blessed,

and that our hearts might rejoice in you.

Hear us and send us.
Enlarge our hearts and bless us.

We ask it, in Jesus' name and for your glory's sake.
Amen.